THE ANCIENT USE OF STONE

the ancient use of stone

JOURNALS AND DAYBOOKS
1998–2008

Ray DiPalma

OTIS BOOKS / SEISMICITY EDITIONS
The Graduate Writing program
Otis College of Art and Design
LOS ANGELES ● 2009

Selections from the six works collected here originally appeared in *Combo, Green Integer Review, The Iowa Review, Lowghost, The New Review of Literature, Sentence, Vanitas, Verse, Vers et proses 1987-2005* (Éditions Virgile), *The Washington Review,* and the Stele Broadside series. To the editors of these publications the author extends his grateful acknowledgment.

I wish to thank the Fund for Poetry for a grant which was of help in writing part of this book.

L'Usage ancien de la pierre, a French translation by Vincent Dussol of the title sequence of this collection was published by Éditions Grèges in 2007.

Special thanks to Vincent Dussol, Lambert Barthélémy, Paul Vangelisti, Douglas Messerli, Elizabeth DiPalma, François Dominique, Dennis Phillips, Ken McCullough, Johnathan Perry, Michael Lally, Merrill Gilfillan, Louis Phillips, Nick Piombino, Thomas Evans, Lisa Jarnot, Emmanuel Hocquard, Juliette Valéry, and Claude Royet-Journoud.

Book design and typesetting: Rebecca Chamlee

ISBN-10: 0-9796177-5-8
ISBN-13: 978-0-9796177-5-1

OTIS BOOKS / SEISMICITY EDITIONS
The Graduate Writing program
Otis College of Art and Design
9045 Lincoln Boulevard
Los Angeles, CA 90045

www.otis.edu
www.gw.otis.edu
seismicity@otis.edu

table of contents

the ancient use of stone

Sia ammazzato chi non porta moccolo!

January 7   [Griffolino d'Arezzo:] "Vedi, Albero, e' sono poche cose ch'io non sappia fare: s'io volessi, io t'insegnerei volare; et s'egli ha in Siena veruna donna a cui tu voglia bene, poterai intrare in casa per le finestre volando." *Commento alla Divina Commedia d'anonimo fiorentino del secolo xiv.*

January 8   Music is restricted to anecdote. "Might as well be walking on the sun." An intimate reticence, to be recorded and later read aloud. No evidence – a system owned – like a by-product.

Original time, believe the projection – watch the fissure spin. I tell you there's light for it. And aire. The scheme from which the rock is abridged. Engaged in constructing an event.

> Engaged in constructing
> A series of events:
> The scheme from which
> The rock is abridged

The inexorable merge missing the membrane of responsibility. "I don't know," he said to the cat. [Only partially visible, 4 PM.]

Hangs from the shoulder. The outcome is exposure, standing doubt, outside the frame. Still, engaged. Thrown.

Take what's under there *out*. Nothing misdirected inside the voice. The struggle of alternation. Penetrated or destroyed?

Written over again [no change between] written over again. The wall [the brick] the wall. The wall [the brick] the wall. The wall [the brick] the wall.

JANUARY 9   More anonymous words. Sirens at the end of extension cords.

What is forgotten? More than half. What will not be remembered? Part of the rest. What is left? Memory's coefficient – some further questions.

Acedia + tristitia. The muck and mire murmur: *tristi fummo*.

January 16 FOVRE LETTERS AND CERTEINE SONNETS: *Especially touching* Robert Greene, and *other parties, by him abused:* But incidently of diuers excellent persons, and some matters of note. *To all courteous mindes, that will vouchsafe the reading.* LONDON Imprinted by Iohn Wolfe, 1592. [Gabriel Harvey]

JANUARY 20   Speculate. *This measure.*

The golden section, Alferi's *Kub Or.* And the reference in *Canto* LXXXVII:

       [and then the "Section", the proportions,]

Broken in the balance –

The specifics of ever-shifting resources

Addressing the words themselves

JANUARY 21   [Sic loquitur equus] Vendetta = comes the debt –

– in libro etymologico –
This friend of a friend . . . tell him for me: "Omnem volve lapidum."

What do we have for memory?
Not merely these *remaining* words.

Contradiction to contradiction to contradiction, held in suspension at right angles to one another. He asked for depth and received grid upon grid variously angled. That, and breath found at the back of the throat.

Hiddenness placed in an arrangement. On its behalf: the focus just another place to begin. The cunning grid, the repeated frame: self absorption.

Whose corners for entropy? Prodigious form?

Mine – or possibly mine.

12:30 AM – A tarantula-sized asterisk and a dog in the hall.

Because of the lifebook they are paving the jungle road ever deeper.

Resolution: Behold the circuit, as wide as the wrist.
Resolution: An extraction.

ANDANTINO: The reminder carefully tapped close to the ear, admirably attentive to a threadbare topic. Ta tata tatatata ta –

JANUARY 22   There is a rhythm to all this. Which to trust? The words? Or the pace of disclosure? The syllables shaped – prefixed, suffixed & the next word & the next – left with that. No peace to be found in the silence. Never. Better face into the wind. Out of what disclosures has it now been further made? There first.

Taunting the oboist.

JANUARY 23   Resolute will. Not to say. Cannot tell from what has been *told*. This scavenzaria! There's a telling, beyond the ship. Which to trust? Cui vide . . . And not in any book. E pensava! He thought. E pensava, caro amico mio. A 'd' rolled in the 'r'.

'Chih' [the word on the page] 'Chung' [its progress]. From base line to horizon – from the last man standing to the remark – what to do with this vestige? Another ghosted owl. Où sont? M. would say there's nothing in all this saying, better to tell you something about something surrounded by an effective arrangement of something and something else. The bitter experience or the rendered smile. All things are made relative by being placed in a larger context. The expression of one is the exclusion of the other.

JANUARY 26 The THIRDE and last Part of Conny-catching. WITH THE NEW DEVISED knauish Art of of Foole-taking. *The like Cosenages and Villenies never before discouered.* By R.G. Imprinted at London by *Thomas Scarlet* for Cutberd Burbie, and are to be solde at his shoppe in the Poultrie, by S. Mildreds Church. 1592.

By reading this little treatise ensuing, you shall see to what marueylous subtill pollicies these deceiuers have atteyned, and how daylie they practise strange driftes for their purpose.

January 27   GREENES, GROATSWORTH of witte, bought with a million of Repentance. DESCRIBING THE FOLLIE OF YOUTH, THE FALSHOOD OF MAKESHIFTE FLATTERERS, THE MISERIE OF THE NEGLIGENT, AND MISCHIEFES OF DECEIUING COURTEZANS. Written before his death and published at his dyeing request. *Fœlicem fuisse infaustum.* LONDON Imprinted for William Wright. 1592.

In an Iland bounded with Ocean there was sometime a Cittie situated, made riche by Marchandize, and populous by long peace, the name is not mentioned in the Antiquarie, or else worne out by times Antiquitie, what it was it greatly skilles not, but therein thus it happened.

[. . . partly for kindered cheefly for craft . . .]

The Repentance of Robert Greene Maister of Artes. Wherein by himself is laid open his loose life, with the manner of his death. AT LONDON, Printed for Curbert Burbie, and are to be sold at the middle shop in the Poultry, vnder Saint Mildreds Church. 1592

Hell (quoth I) what talke you of hell to me? I know if I once come there, I shal haue the company of better men than my selfe, I shal also meete with some madde knaues in that place, & so long as I shall not sit there alone, my care is the lesse.

*

Qui avoit vielle mere
Mout felonnesse et mout avere;
Bochue estoit, noire et hideuse
Et de touz biens contralieuse.
Tout li mont l'avoit contre cuer,
Li prestres meisme a nul fuer
Ne vosist pour sa desreson
Qu'el entrast ja en sa meson;
Trop ert parlant et de pute ere

*

I had learned to think much and bitterly before my time .... Talk not of the bitterness of middle-age and after life; a boy can feel all that, and much more, when upon his young soul the mildew has fallen; and the fruit, which with others is only blasted after ripeness, with him is nipped in the first blossom and bud. And never again can such blights be made good; they strike in too deep, and leave such a scar that the air of Paradise might not erase it.

—Melville, *Redburn*

January 28   Follow the vein. Dig, clear, and stope it out. Without story or program notes. The record written in *moumia*, a mix of wax and tallow, on a parchment of camel's skin.

The same said and the terms of the saying: *hie, kotan, karabi – cold, icy beauty, simplicity, and austere, monochromatic dryness.*

'He seldom speaks; he loathes conversation, he spurns news of any kind, he shrinks from strangers . . .' [Beckford, Alcobaça & Batalha]

Souvenirs or splinters, accumulations of data, selected prejudices – gathering at the core. My route from *Kaf to Kaf.*

To be entered sideways, but still facing East. How does it look from in there? Two turns. And now? Are you still facing East? There should be enough light to perceive the wave-knot cresting the far wall.

Grapes, olives, and figs.
Acorns, dried fish, and pomegranates.

What part of the past the series dictates writ small?

Descriptive, momentary variables – *ko* [   ] *tan*

The contents of the frame turned to a right angle against the
horizon – spadework.
The contents of the frame turned at a right angle across the horizon – each according to its own time. The *respective.* Eye beyond eye.

An *auditor* who never made more than a very brief visit to the systematic – no such thing as an excellent summary – that being their words –

JANUARY 29   The perception of impropriety invigorated by a sense of novelty –

Trying to account for an existence
Reconciliation is effected only at the level of intellect

Difference – the subsequent spaces – confirmed by bone inscriptions

The obvious earth and broken sky – new evidence passed along – that burden
found waiting in the books no one knew you had.

Through the trees
the smell of burning pine
blue smoke across the moon
reflected in a rockpool

January 30 Ruminative, something very fine to murmur, but not explain. An aptitude for what takes shape beyond the page.

... *age-old nomadic customs ... [their] objects and associated rituals.*

Wrapped in felt.

Allocutions. Tales of traders. The cryptic mention of attributes. The thread turned and pulled. Not without reason. Adjacent strategies. Hallucinatory and skeptical. Some unravelled, some detachable part.

FEBRUARY 2   Factive. A search for convictions. Long shadows at sunset, run according to a persistent and inexplicable mathematics. No amelioration. Nothing sweetened [a-mel]. The hand never extended by any party. Therefore, not a casual perusal of attributions, not a carefully contrived delineation, but a mathematics. How angled the arc of either tropic?

One can go too far in humouring pedants and fanatics for colloquial speech when printing one's thought. [GUIDE TO KULCHUR]

I am drawn to wonder . . . I will try another way.

Erasing all that is transparent, in anticipation of intuition. Added *out.*
Sleepless rhythms. Centered on black. [Luna *see* moon, the]

Denouncing all that is ungenerous and amended – patterns and silhouettes glued to cheap cardboard and called patina – thought of as the spoils of secured alignments. The windows closed, the drapes drawn, the lights dimmed, the doors locked – all the detachment of cash. No sleep, the watchface is iced over.

A dead bird tied to the end of a kite string –
Maybe a polonaise, between terrific shouts,
Or a sad fit of coughing behind the pinball machine –
The local loco: eyebrows? No, a mask. Signed, *El Looneyoso*

*

Cables & pavement
Careful Egyptian ways

Cranium (dolichocephalic)
Capacity: 1700 cubic centimeters

Compliments: none
Construct: mere nomination

Complexity: plain enough
Carbon anchoring this

Chih 止
Choice and caveat

February 3   *. . . a relationship to objects that does not emphasize their functional, utilitarian value – that is, their usefulness – but studies and loves them as the scene, the stage, of their fate.*
        —Walter Benjamin

Decay, the many approaches to "before very long" read anachronistically.

Barn wood, stripped doors, broken windows, loose clapboard, abandoned function.

A suppression of scale. Tact, singularity . . . conversion. A village of stone huts thrown against a hillside.

Frescos excavated from a necropolis. No objects, only the terms of the architecture. Mutely expressive. Of the time not the time – *now* in time. One different story.

The liberty of word that poetry confers is poetry's technique, not truth's. [THE TELLING]

Beyond the clatter of the keys. "Vedi, Albero . . ." the faint echo persists. Purpose, a splinter's intersection with the pleasured end of a sentence – emptiness answered with a street. Someone's there. Billowing; out of the woods. Walking; through the changes, listening to the darkness.

February 4 A trajectory inscribed. But at what point along the arc? The integrity of lesser objects, unnamed. More than as many – a measure, *zum Beispiel*. And a measure *of*. A representation of hostile origins. What has collected behind the hands. *Al poco giorno e al gran cerchio d'ombra / In the small hours with the darkness describing a huge circle* – no better place in which to stand . . . *e al gran cerchio d'ombra* pulled around me – having wandered there – περιπλους – to be taken up, grasped by the ring piercing the lobe of the left ear –

[At a bitten angle]

Words written down
Be Advised

The Red Folder
Its contents added-up

[This corner made by a magpie]

*

Is there an index
The approval of certain things

Just a reflection
Come a piece at a time

– As was unlikely
Inadequate or not

*

Not circumscribed but circumscribing all

A low line of purple hills unmarred by human habitation

Part of a song of loss and regret

FEBRUARY 5   Peculiar utterances in the main. Recorded with the edge, not
the point of the pen. These distinctions must be made – rain, sleet, and
snow – someone might be listening. Never got much but a thirst for it; and the
silence that pursued being occasionally well answered. A lot, in part, of what we
only have time for.

Exactly what the mind registers. Nocturnal sounds. For which X has no answer.
They could speak and I could listen. Then I could speak and you could listen.
Then we could speak. Owing to any sense of wonder, whatever might come next.
Ελικοβλεφαρε – quick glancing. Owing to *any*. Leads to assessment.

Along another metropolitan corridor, snow a hundred miles to the north, rain a
hundred miles to the south.

*

Abstractions, follies, and illusions – domani, paisano . . . domani –
glosses and nexi – *una vita sbagliata* –

Those strange people, names that cannot be spoken,
Faces and voices, crowding about . . . dispersed

Complicit, narrowing – "redactions and epitomes"
Nothing but a few spoken words.

This much variety – a story
Much different from that now on record

Words in their correct order, accents properly placed
Let the nourishment fit the crime

FEBRUARY 9   Brief cento:

>The fount of gentle speech yields answer meet,
>So that the deed and the sweet words be one.

*

Plectrum fallen into a pot of ink –

>. . . enriched by the toil of those who have gone before. [M]
>. . . that they be not degraded by any accident. [DVE]

Localization: self-taught. The reputation of the response –
Circular motion symbolizes faultless activity.
    The world still feels like winter.

FEBRUARY 10   Alliances – on the periphery

And right below	Its elementarity
No doubt	A voracious clarity
Minutely layered	Subject to what X
Parabolic reiteration	Will not tell me
Longitudinal perdition	But decides and proposes
Speaks and says " Spoken and said"	Again and again

Concerned with more than the field across which we look
And disclose at the same time

Colonnades
No space for the page

Contentious **carbonization**

Nothing about its reduction but its surge
LITOTEMIC

Smoothing back anything that would adhere
Restricted in its gain – without an increase in sound

FEBRUARY 11 What counts is what's written down – nothing to be said until then. Nothing to extend the half hour. Only the ice-scratch. Resurrected in predicament. Head held back, lest the words fall out of his nose.

They hunt for sentiments to fit into their vocabulary. [EP]

For there are more letters in all languages not communicated
For there are some that have the power of sentences. O rare
  thirteenth of March 1761.
For St Paul was caught up into the third heavens.
For there he heard certain words which it was not possible for him
  to understand.
For they were constructed by uncommunicated letters.
For they are signs of speech too precious to be communicated for ever.

—JUBILATE AGNO

*

FOREST AND CAVE

The book is an album
not a final set of solutions

The real discoveries
Are to be found elsewhere

What the book exhibits
Are the ways to them

*

[I] In consideration. In despite.
[502. "What sentence?"]

[II] MATTER
Grammar & physics

*

Totality: a selection from all the intervals.
Infinity: the time to make a selection.

What might eventually be arrived at? [Via x to x.]
Only particular parts, concentric.

*

[Apropos *January Zero*]:

69. Isn't it like this: a phenomenon (specious present) contains time, but isn't in
time.
  It's form is time, but it has no place in time.
  Whereas language unwinds in time.
—*Philosophical Remarks*

*

Codex – a map of auspicious places – its array
Gateway to gateway.
Unentered – earning what it says. And abandons.

How far does the writ extend in order to establish a pattern?
The length and width of the vein: though misled by analogies –
Undetermined variations scaling the dial –

A continuous transition difficult to negotiate
– The reach obtrudes
Any part of the straight line that establishes the curve

The mark that distinguishes the materials
From the preferred solutions –
Launching and overtaking the first context

A ligature established and sustained beyond any formula

Something dislodged and turned upside down

FEBRUARY 12   Not veneer – heartwood. Descriptive signatures. The purely descriptive *spoken at* the demonstrable. Sayable, therefore of secondary importance. An exclusionary perspective shaped by what has been brought about and turned to.

Savoring a lack of emphasis, while misunderstanding any progressing aspect of a possibility. Misdirection. As discoverable by . . . Beyond assent. This will be set out by what has been set upon. The aggressions of form. Beyond suggestion or shared regulative assent within the congering subtleties of paradigm.

*

In a crude box of stone. Ostensives. Bones.

The materials: an observable legacy.
The simplest and the most problematic.

A portion of distance the water embossed.

*

Appraisal of validity – and with of.

Affirmed only within a portion of its fullness – an aspect that would enlarge upon what is only partially knowable – then protracted and retracted throughout whatever theoretical bias has been established.

Once again, not the thought but the thinking, lost with the sphinx's tail.

*

Hypothesizing primary losses and gains
Postulating primary losses and gains

"I discovered and ventured divers answers; I distinguished between ages, peoples, degrees of rank among individuals; I departmentalized my problem; out of my answers there grew new questions, inquiries, conjectures, probabilities – until at length I had a country of my own, a soil of my own, an entire discrete, thriving, flourishing world, like a secret garden the existence of which no one suspected."

—On the Genealogy of Morals

*

"Poems should echo and reecho against each other. They should create resonances. They cannot live alone any more than we can."

"Things fit together. We knew that – it is the principle of magic. Two inconsequential things can combine together to become a consequence. This is true of poems too. A poem is never to be judged by itself alone. A poem is never by itself alone."

—*Admonitions*

Put back on the way down the hall
– Thus, thus, and so

The point of this last remark, etc
So many, and several others

The same traps

February 13 Tangle after tangle, as is the custom. The neglect of and arrival by the second guess. "What's ragged should be left ragged." [L.W.]

. . . landowners have a way with words.

[The embeddedness of grammar and history –]*This is also why we cannot see our own noses – they're all on the moon.* —Gogol

The collective representation before and after – directed integration – indices and solutions – some and sum – allowing the limits.

Oneiric disjunction and anecdote – a balancing act for parlance. Parole + payroll. The nail floats. How heavy is the water?

Neglected Orchards

Bracketing both the *Anfang* and anything deeply coded. First wave to last wave, the undertow. Die Angabe: der Anfall und der Andrang und der Anerbe und der Angang. [Angebot und Nachfrage]. Kein 'ihr' – keines . . . Only when and where we hide the gear – *Also sprach homo ludens*

*

The supplicant minima of an integration taken into the hand [UNAUTHORIZED VERSION]. Instance delivers formula & verb supposes examples in space. [AUTHORIZED VERSION].

The mask of isolation: a hinge to see through.

Hammertongue provides symmetry &
Mœbius the triangular loop

Abstracting what might only be aggregate –

A diagram with attached provisos –
Moving not through levels but frontiers

Refracted to dust
The reckoning an unreachable state of matter
Tho still a part of an alphabet
Unsettled incomprehensible remembering

FEBRUARY 15 Foraging among ominous plumes. Discovering valid sources other than the historical record. Hiding among the draperies and book-strewn furniture . . . a fire in the kitchen, where the names of birds still have their place.

*

ISABELLA AND THE POT OF BRAMBLES

Under a mortal cloud
The common perfection

Blue brows and
A clutch of possibilities

Uneven fanfares
And short-term mythologies

Bent double, nose to the mandolin
About to become a psychic distance

The dance and when the music flags
The sign for the dance

Folds and elevations –

February 16 *Alternative drafts, partial erasures, repetitions, and additions . . .* No final form. What remains is approximate and mutually exclusive. There should ever be only two copies.

Dry, cold, moist, or hot –

Sanguine, hot and moist, Air
Choleric, hot and dry, Fire
Melancholy, cold and dry, Earth
Phlegmatic, cold and moist, Water

[. . . a learned store of ethical precept culled from many ancient authorities.]

Let Nepheg rejoice with Cenchris which is the spotted serpent.
For I bless God in the libraries of the learned and for all the booksellers
  in the world.

         —JUBILATE AGNO, Fragment B

Sentimental, ill-tempered, and enormous
And this distinction –
The distractions of great bones, gleaming blackness, and enormous frowns
A permission for death and nothing ornamental

FEBRUARY 17 "Leave no widows." He was the most honest man I ever met; in consequence of which he was of no use to anyone. ["Vedi, Albero . . .]

By "frame" he meant his body— Ankles, all ankles. Wise and silent, the coldblooded starts here. Pathetic and bronze, something to walk past on the way to lunch. Motioning from deep within a mysterious and noiseless endurance, it remains a showpiece blocking the aisle no matter where it's placed.

The ms. was lost and pieces were scattered everywhere. The search for original pages goes on to this day. Soothing iotas—something that can be built only from what has been left behind. That degree of intelligence usually missing from anything rhapsodic. Humming and confessing, sporadic internal noises, effigies and comparisons. One set of instruments explaining matters to another set of instruments. Who said why to whom? Nostalgia, doubts, and rumors all beside the point. The parlance you need, the parlance you put your mind to.

*

VERITAS etched on the bi-focal
in 7 point type

The weed in the dogma
Supports the late harvest

Menial vigor kept moving
To emerge from the smoke

Diamonds tumbled
With clods of frozen sand

February 18   Edge, the only unity. Turned out to stare at the broken columns. An infinite number of sloping lines dropped into a signature. Intuited from the point of the tower to the small black stone on the table in the corner of the room.

Ten or fifteen words organized around two or three marks of punctuation.

Else – the other side
Else – a point, a large hole

*

Sentences in ink
Sentences in light

Red wheels beneath the track across the mirror
At the edge of the field

Yellow
In which a system of touch is
Suspended in copies of yellow

A little more of the distance
Shadow across shadow

What is not in its place
What is missing

The fidelity of a
Motionless egg

*

THE ROBOT & THE NAKED MAN [25 YEARS LATER]

A more aggressive neutrality is expected
From the mechanical marvel standing in the corner
Wrapped in white and left on the stairs
Everything analyzed by sound
Its particle nature in fine amounts named gathered and hidden
Captions on a spool in conversation with and more receptive to
An undetermined science and whatever else might lie just ahead
A symmetry of shadows extends through the ones it casts
Unclear what was lost clear where the loss took place

FEBRUARY 19   "Oaths are the fossils of piety." -Santayana

In an attempt to transcend my limitations I have thought to create an expressive neutrality. These pages I give to the dog to shred.

*

MARBLE SHOES

'I have not brought
the message. I came
with the message.

I am a part of what
is said to have
happened.'

*

Pauses or deletions in the text: ainos (story) & ainigma

". . . an abstract unity . . ." [Baudelaire]:
and the unapproachable distance.

"All research on the labyrinth ought properly to begin with the dance." [Kerenyi]

An inevitable order in the world
Compels silence

Not an outcome but a simulacrum
Of its rhythm

A Physiologie

Divisions by folio
increment is shrugged into convention
Stock still and lacking the immediate
it stretches through the inconspicuous until
the undifferentiated and meditative appear
Supple and resistant and as attentive as unheard
amark on the erasable floor
What thought would you give
to the thought you would give –
disputing abstractions
non plus modes under foot
in ruling out the perfected space around anything attached –
divining the obstinate and axial

*

Poem

Blindfolded and consoled
he stood beside the blackened cabinet
where the monument had occurred – the moon,
barbed wire, buttons of limestone, dirt, and ice –
succinct and equidistant

Another cigarette another whiskey *in extremis*
explained the private leagues and fathoms of dent –

Amnesia and a footprint over the sigh
co-opt the nightly report
invite concern for a spotless record

Had it been colder, had it been thicker
it might have worked better

February 23   L'autre jour, facing the rectangle painted in red and silver . . . During the course of the day a man arrived from X – bringing with him several small clay tablets, papyri, and inscribed parchments. These he had wrapped in linen and hidden among his undergarments. Some months later I heard he contracted fever and died at Aleppo. As I seem to remember.

Even now the upheavals of the Thirty Years War continue to drive me from place to place. But these journeys provide many documents; and their fame spreads through the desert. Eau d'eau.

The fifth edition (I have no way of knowing whether it is the most recent) has been opened and zealously circulated. A corrective hand extends from a series of minor but still somewhat pertinent FACTS. Sheltered in a tall narrow structure having neither doors nor windows. And beyond that a small temple.

The icon's enormous gaze fits into a small silver spoon. Eyes, forehead, cheekbones, and the mouth. All distinctly gathered within the bowl of a tiny silver spoon. The light from the votive candle underneath the frame washes out all other detail. Repenting of the optimism it once commanded. Caught midway between an incisive summary and an indignant sense of dread, denial seeks its unique shape out of an effective balance of these terms. Primitive singularities abound. The standard depiction on the label of the magic bottle offers practiced installments of ardor the potable contents failed to clarify and advance.

[Here the manuscript breaks off.] As I seem to remember.

FEBRUARY 24 Yesterday . . . Nothing further to add about the effects of the weather. Breathing the numerical, satisfied in order to live. The enigma of affection that epitome renders speechless. As logical as the chemistry and the music applied. Slowly through the fog. Anything linear running against the rain and rays of sunlight starting to pierce the fog. As though there were some narrow advantage to word after word – or word before word – breathing again in a state of deftly manipulated desire. Footfalls along some emergency – an evenness and smoothness drawn into the purpose. One reverberates; one descends – believing such distinctions were necessary. Used up within the result.

FEBRUARY 25

THEIR FORM THEIR INFINITY

Perched immobile, short of breath
A by-the-way launched into the matter-of-fact
I can't remember what it was –
Mentioned, motioned, concocted
Repetitive approaches reveal – space

Explanation: reconstructing the coincidence –
Machine-made, flattened, forgotten
Seeking common ground
The Bronze Age serves as first point of reference
Black scratches in gold – small bright creatures
Located in their convictions

Then lost in sleep
With conversation elevated to a conversation:
Someone in a brick hat towers into the late afternoon sunlight –
Scattered applause, wood against wood, shuffling feet, squealing hinges,
Slamming doors, shattering glass, ripping cloth, muffled screams.
Texture and clarity. Second feature followed by a newsreel, three cartoons,
    and a serial.

Tomorrow only: Episode 3: ZEPPELIN OF DOOM

*

CUNNING

Magnanimous evasions and strategies meticulously violated,
Forgotten conflicts, maxims, wily distractions, sonorities,
Logical starting points, garbled melodies, dissemblings,
Perpetual adjustments, baffling embraces, panaceas, trills,
Recapitulations, subverted calibrations, drifting rhythms,
Aimless tracings, slogans, requisite materials, hybrids, puzzles,
Penalties, nuances, seductive myths, targets, elegant solutions,
Adornments, disparate etymologies, routines, cavalier methods,
Complex interpretations, jargons, weird polarities, chosen dialects,
Melancholias, bravura caprices, abbreviations, masquerades

FEBRUARY 26 Historians, translators and penitents digging trenches, writing postcards. Calculations, clever strides – no more analytic rummage – fundamentals large and stock-still; the agency of moods in objection declaiming the chainlink, putting titles to choice, enhancing the fashion to read sudden exits as aggressive behavior. New precedents stick to where it's rough – the search for instructions establishes the fabric of predictability – thinking of the thought then adding the words. Where the modulations straighten, add more primary seductions; where they sag, direct the glare and read everything as the effects of metaphor.

*

TRAVERSAL OF RESIDUA

To the = radius of spills
With the = shapes behind the glass
By the = limits of virtual syntax
For the = and the
On the = under the

*

OTHER VERSIONS

Number *waits*
A step in any direction

Replacing the variation
With a plus or minus

———————————

Number *waits*
With a plus or minus

A step in any direction
Replacing the variation

February 27

de travail, de beau travail d'hiver

What remain
are the edges of pursuit, the accidents of detail –
the flat phrases of the oracle indicating only shortness of breath
– the weight of the name fixes the leads – the bared measure
keeping watch on three pieces of the hour

MARCH 2

THREE INSCRIPTIONS

I

The urn used by the temple priests is empty
But something long dormant is on the rise again

The portion we have was left to gravity
A bittersweet account voluntarily postponed

It remained under 1500 feet of bedrock

Sealed within the displacements of its shadows

The smooth is equal to the unusual
An argument offered by the broken lattice

A disclosure from the unseen past
Fades into an invocation of its form

II

Menace has a grand design
An almost scriptural breadth
This division of its limitations
Possesses a generative force
More complex than the confinements
Of its disorder reveal

Unaware of its dedications
The attempted recomposition of its demands
And overtures – the scoring of its terms –
Reinstate a circumstantial vocabulary
Skewed by its genesis

Because these are exclusive desires
Only echoes remain
The reduced effect of insistence
As opposed to character

III

The choir maintains its axioms
With suspiciously precise fractions
Its earnestness is full of exhausted irony
Confusing the lyrical with the profound

A syllable sleeps in the rose filling the eye
It stays half a tone louder than the syllable asleep in the ear
Another story deferred to the optic
Reduced to the respiratory

An integral part of what continues to be uncertain
Devotion obscures all loyalty to the gesture
A contradicted judgement settled by the tongue
It emerges in deference to a chain of causality
An entelechy of events averred through descending levels of intention

Perspective is always a jagged line

March 4   *The Letters of Nikolai Gogol* – " . . . looking rather preoccupied, he would suddenly return to his room and add a few words to the manuscript."

*

"One of their treatments was to surround his body with warm loaves of bread."

MARCH 9

ACROSS THE DESERT TO LA

Torture arson murder madness and greed

Earlier, when the ink was thinner,
I was ruining my eyes in bad light as a favor to you
In a belief that the best opportunities are exacted from the dark

I was given new maps every day
To prevent news of my arrival
From reaching any further than the next hill

I always knew you'd be there
Waiting with the door half-open
And all the lights on upstairs

Languishing with some bad news
At the end of a few well connected thoughts
When a more comprehensive perspective was what was needed

So I turned and faced the man on the hill
Who was sketching the battle from memory
Assumption and conviction had come to mean the same thing for both of us

He thought he should put something down on paper
Here near the top of the page
Lest you think his work was of some personal interest to anyone

MARCH 10 Home life with tea leaves and a dog. Where bowls of blossoms and stacks of books meet the blue and green mountains and every conversation begins "I've been meaning to tell you." A fragile, ingratiating life. Its occulted goal a minor achievement.

Interests at the center of any enterprise invariably concern privilege, not the elimination of contradictions. Lithe in its effort. The of that departs from the or. Latent and retractable it motions, prompted by depth, to become a vacant symmetry. Black, timid, and sour. The stinking breath of a welcoming conscience confirms a morose expertise. Any apprehending rules and contradictions dissolve in a carpet of vapors.

MARCH 11

IRONY'S EAVESDROP

Recording a disaffection with self-surveillance
on a semantic level it functions in the same way again and again

As expression it lacks any other strategic primacy

MARCH 12

Having not yet found a satisfactory explanation,
Men moved in gathering columns toward the horizon, eyes wide open

Their myth, premonitory and marginal,
Is a meretricious one

MARCH 13   Affirmations are invariably tested, but always in the dark.

Discourse transforms possibility
into endless function

Function transforms discourse
into endless possibility

The face in the wall
absorbing the imaginary terms of its tributes

Tyromachia

MARCH 14 [Maze and frieze motifs]

Before the river tributaries
and before the backroads that ran along them were formed

Where powerful alliances were made
and uncertain transitions

The wind stops
15 centuries old

A shadow hiding us
with increasing reluctance
from the moonlight

MARCH 15 "The best part of human language, properly so called, is derived from reflections on the acts of the mind itself." [Coleridge]

"The sum, of human wisdom is not contained in any one language, and no single language is capable of expressing all forms and degrees of human comprehension." [Ezra Pound]

Citation *enacts* the agency of specific material within a new and larger context. Its aspect comprises more than a *frame* of reference.

MARCH 19 A nostalgia for preestablished harmony philosophically rendered –

The lapse (containment – its placement in time) and applicable resonance modulate which? Nostalgia? Preestablished harmony? Or the TESTIMONY of "for" –

Participating in – MOVING through – all that has been *removed* –
Conceiving, stylizing, and allowing the record to be made: the only approbation: indifference and escape – WITHOUT THEIR APPROPRIATE HESITATION

MARCH 20   Winding up the process and the tempo good and tight – and winding up the winder – convinced as far as – up to and past the zero –

19. Why is it that something can be transparent green but not transparent white?

   Transparency and reflection exist only in the dimension of depth of a visual image.

   The impression that the transparent medium makes is that something lies *behind* the medium. If the visual image is thoroughly monochromatic it cannot be transparent.

36. Whatever *looks* luminous does not look grey. Everything grey *looks* as though it is being illuminated.

44. We speak of a 'black' mirror. But where it mirrors, it darkens, of course, but it doesn't look black, and that which is seen in it does not appear 'dirty' but 'deep'.

45. Opaqueness is not a *property* of the white colour. Any more than transparency is a property of the green.

—Wittgenstein, Remarks on Colour

Silence and color. Language and black and white.

MARCH 23   A chronology – the ingredients of a story – a roped-off space, well lit – occasions where detail erases detail –

Long distances reduced to messages
written in the ashes and the snow

gridando il padre a lui "Mala via tieni!"

only the sound of an old name spoken
in the cluttered alleys near the tracks

that run behind the mills
stretching along the river

MARCH 24   A crease of light pushes and extends the radius as far as the center of town – the domain of the extra intruder, the size of whose descendents [any known to be alive] is resurrection – hauled away altogether, uncle and brother, sister and son

One after one
the pivot agrees
with the occasion
of its circle
– splitting
the balance
                another
either way one
more or less
returning
the substance
of its claim

MARCH 25

1
mogul's horizontals
plugged with the directional

2
he explains an acceptance
the transmutation of silence

3
which is which *while*
the acceptance or the transmutation

4
and which while *while*
the explanation or the silence

5
not the occasion declared either
by which *while* or which while *while*

6
or the = DECLARING THE SCRUTINY
AND THE EXPANSION OF CONSEQUENCE

7
what the residual harkens –
a matter for another page

8
stock: syntax, punctuation, num-
bers, typography, arrows, lines

9
deployment: taxonomy's
                  hyphen

10
the concerns of the splay
more sculptural than painterly

March 26

Orthography

Scoured, iconic, and unduly gracious
I must return to all these developments
and not to the familiarity of a shelter hidden
just beyond the stand of trees –
a single room lit with an oil lamp and furnished
with a wooden chair and a zinc-top table

With the assumption of this stance
it has become difficult to miss the deceptiveness of the source
and the changes that have emerged
as readily as photographic evidence

Singled out, fallen short of the realities,
the question has arisen of how this happens –
its ontology realized only in terms of detachment
metamorphosis emerges only in contradiction –
regret, nostalgia, or loss become a gesture for that limit

MARCH 27   Comment was the best model – committed to the largely
invisible – the stimulus of damage was obscured in the rush to say something
remarkable and immediate – the contortions of clairvoyance set in motion
by the barest suggestion of rhythm – a persistent infatuation – a reckless
illusion – merely a way of saying they entered the room – the only imperative not
not in motion –

Half a mile wide
No moonlight

The silent river
Shaded by trees

"Sawyers"
Shoptaw explains

MARCH 29   "...a mixture of privation and infinity..." [E.M. Cioran on *Lessness*]

The terms: remote, strange, unfamiliar, frightening, unpredictable, and real.

Written in grey ink.

A perspective based on the lack of any fossil evidence.

Beyond any set of conventional distinctions
by which to render method –

So water trembling in a polish'd vase
Reflects the beam that plays upon its face,
The sportive light, uncertain where it falls,
Now strikes the roof, now flashes on the walls.

> *The Aeneid*, Book VIII (trans. by Wm Cowper)

March 30

10,000 Feet above and 2000 Feet Below

Many pages mysteriously disappeared before they could be typeset
Discussion improved the little that was spared
Fragrance and gravity were recorded somewhere further down
And were meant only to regulate certain predilections
Anticipated but not yet specifically determined
Certain pages such as 451, 455, 463-67, 474, 479, 515, 546, and 557
Many of which had been left blank
Perhaps as some unidentifiable investment in the future
Such as the next time the moon was a crescent above the mausoleum
Formed another part of the story

MARCH 31

NOTES OF A BOO HOW DOY

I arrive an alert minstrel of the apothegm
Articulator of distraction's liturgy
Ready to trade songs

Like rhetoric in a narration of the eye —
To loosen a receptive element from the listening hum
As invasive as the echo of an after-gong

"And soon ripe, soon rotten . . ."
For its disorder nothing known
But ever expected the only certainty

To fulfill the apprehensions of the next idea transfixed
By trope and secret commonplace

I stand in the dark and sing

April 1

1
At a right angle
to the heaped boundary

As far forward as the strategy
and the light will allow

This is the tongue of the weave

2
A circumspection
of movements dissolving in aptitude –
errata usurping any call of judgement

Larger than further away
smaller than nearer at hand

The execution of the circle

3
The mark refuses the ambiguity of its own grace
Shrewdly intricate it relinquishes
the signs and numbers of mishap and abiding calm

Cherished asperities and undisturbed counterfeits

4
Four black keys and three white
for the edge aside and the divagations of the thaw

Eye-deep in a record to be set straight
the custom of strong opinion is mistaken for a warning

An axis untangles no roots

5
A mirage in the distance for emphasis

April 2

Bird tongues all speaking piano
None saltier than the splash of ink

Acrid pink and chrome
Where the sun sets

The Jack of Diamonds
Breathed into the ruby

A guest of the missing
Leaned and looked and spoke in growls

A mixture of syllables and nimble appraisal
Put like an anthem

Outside in the cold the lapis steam
Advertises shoeshine and chop suey

APRIL 3   All the texts of pilgrimage maintained the valid designations. A self-interrupting apologia comprising brief exclamations and anonymous voices full of responsibility and foreboding – inserted and over-inked, minus the mysteries of exposure. The almost perfect answer, heard farthest from.

*

ISLAND LIFE: DAY TO DAY

The sun's a floating stone. No?
Sepia pre-lit, ochre lit – off on – on off –
Probative work, where the light opens on the edge of the rain.

Right foot down, left foot still in the air – where is the boundary?
Zu Fuß, still advancing still unraveling how many years the river has been flowing
Across the realigned fragments of territory.

Horse and bird, grass, food, and pearls all for transaction,
My little darkening flock has its day set aside in the ***Almanac Joie,***
Badly printed on cheap paper – white, almost at the risk of transparency.

Exhausted by anticipation, I took out a knife,
A cutting board, and the remains of a ten day old loaf of bread.
I was going to make something for the birds.

APRIL 5   [NOTES FOR THE RAVINE]

Carried at the point of balance
Nullified by the weight of the book
The diagonal moon
Shapes touching the glass
Poison under the floor
The tiles one by one
All the expected places
With a 3 hour head start
Secrecy as a solution to the problem
A bowl full of nails
Curious beyond intimacy
Working in silence
No longer limited to extorting
The plain of the marginal
Horizontal relationships
In fragments
Quasimathematical
Surveillance and its spectators
Minimal equivalence attaining solution
Delivery not conversion
Particular controls
Isolations and system drift
Working forward of the light
Across the corners
Blunting the anticipation of the angle
Compelled by knots and waves
Steep acoustics
A duplicate direction without repeating
This NEXT is the DEAD and this PRIME is the END
A reed and an oblong stone
Else unedited unelse read

APRIL 7 What comprises a self-important assessment of serenity, or an imagined record of same? A summarizing, come as a reaction singular to disenchantment at a time of cautious leave-taking. Stones falling off the roof, nails driven only part way into the boards – far from where you are – in some other place where impatience, conjured by real mysteries, asserts its curiosity and randomness. Like the weather it continues to self-correct – offering an imperfect limit, one with no depth, but only lacking an afterthought, additional information of which you remain unaware. No resignation, no inertia, but a radical realigmenmt of the only part of life that has come down to us – absence. Every exclamatory 'O' an eye closed on the proceedings. It turns away corrupted by its own music. The heart of the matter a common currency devalued a whisper at a time. A final greeting difficult to record.

APRIL 8   *The skull forward* COMPLETED. Contraband. Allotments. As were the words. Time road [EPOCH] exacting perpetual [EPOCH TO EPOCH] bird light. A phrase, 5 or 6 words, enough to lift a truck out of the mud. A measure of possible completeness. To make an answer. The missing part of nature. The words, like a figure in a painting resting against the space around it, changing color.

EXPECT TEMPERATURES TODAY IN THE MID-50S TO LOW 60S WITH A MIX OF SUN AND CLOUDS AND A 40 PERCENT CHANCE OF LIGHT RAIN IN THE LATE AFTERNOON OR EARLY EVENING. WINDS ARE OUT OF THE WEST AT 7 MILES AN HOUR. HUMIDITY IS AT 90 PERCENT. THE POSSIBILITY OF STRONG THUNDERSTORMS AND HEAVY DOWNPOURS EXISTS AFTER MIDNIGHT. CERTAIN LOW-LYING AREAS MAY EXPERIENCE FLOODING. RAIN WILL BE HEAVIEST ALONG THE SHORE. SOME BEACH EROSION CAN BE EXPECTED.

A distant echo, as unlimited as unnoticed. Another one-way street. Wire over wire – a coppery shine that excludes chance. An arrangement of solitary reserves: turning to look back, hoarding word upon word, bright, almost warm, charting the sulks. A rich harvest at the back of the century where okay signals okay.

APRIL 9 "The important thing about a word is not the sound in itself, but those phonic differences which allow this word to be distinguished from other words, for it is these which are the bearers of meaning." [Roman Jakobson]

NEURAL MIRAGE AND SHADOW GEOMETRIES

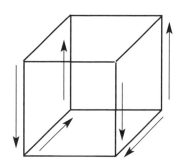

His signal consisted of a protracted series of complicated hand gestures, meant to portray time in 2 pages

WILL HAVE BEEN

traces a long process

heavier by a declarative nuance

an archive of never made judgements

thoroughness uncollated

the distortion

the original – which disappears

component, addendum
not paradigm

UNTIL

renders complete
for some reason or *then*

the reflection
before and after

change seemed in memory

REPRODUCTION

otherwise struck dumb

become something to be

placed between overlapping shadows

to mark time between the original distance

and the light it accumulated

APRIL 10 Only at the solstice would they tell us what they believe they can leave behind; not as a justification but as a way of saying – adding that though now dissociated, all is meant to be found again in the same versions at a much later date; however, in quite different contexts and produced exactly as they had been 400 years ago, but whose original models had been hidden at least a further 300 hundred years prior.

*

To move about is to define

Things to do generating things to say
        generating things to be done

Convictions to be extricated and identified

As though the measured were no longer among the discarded
Or return confused with about to enter

Where were the words that left a certain smell on the hands
That made the ears sensitive and eased
The pressure on the eyes

Blank glass scrolls
Their scratches filled with ink

A music of smoke and anise
The stolen name fills an entire page

A compendium of assimilated errors
Rounded by calm

Decaying arabesques

Enumerations of a mongrel detachment

[1998]

jihadgraphy

Raids are our agriculture.

—BEDOUIN PROVERB

Discuss 'Summerhill' briefly with R—. "Freedom encourages fearlessness." Later in the day, coincidentally, find a heavily marked copy of A.S. Neill's book in a thrift shop at 8th & 21st—my old Chelsea neighborhood. A block and a half west of the bldg where most of my classes meet this term.

Prepared 4 e-mails over the last few days with extensive notes & clarifications for Vincent apropos his initiating a translation of *The Ancient Use of Stone*.

E-mail from François Dominique telling me I shd remind Legrand that we have a contract & money has changed hands—he is therefore legally bound to publish *Lettres* whether CNL provides Virgile with funding or not.

Leave NYC for Hudson in the late afternoon. When we get there, a Christmas postcard from Merrill is in the mailbox—postmarked prior to December 25, 2001, it obviously took more than 4 weeks to arrive. Perhaps due to some anthrax-related delay. I plan to call him in Boulder, but decide not to do so. Look for my copy of *In Our Time* and various critical books on Hemingway and Faulkner located at the farm. They all turn up where I remembered shelving them. Decide on a brief discussion of 'courtly love' in connection with "A Rose for Emily" as a way into the story. A theme suggested briefly by Brooks in his book on Faulkner.

Dream Images: Asian female face, doll like, unreal—more than a mask, large square head, smooth flesh tones: uniformly bright pinkish-orange, small mouth speaking of what is *not* permissible. Evocative of Lindner sculptures. More Lindner than Helmut Newton. Carefully detailed, but unreal. Nothing distinctive about the timbre of the voice. But the expressed nature of what is not allowed has a generalized field of referents rather than a directly particularized one. What is not permitted? What is transgressive in this encounter? Whose voice(s)? Recall something Creeley said at a reading at Simon's Rock 10 years ago about how all the characters and their voices are really those of the dreamer and *only* the dreamer. "We are not allowed. = They would strongly prefer that we not do so." All in a large open room in a private club organized around a series of landscape paintings. Amply but subtly lit. Couches. One on one. Who for whom? The London club and situation described in chapter 46 of *Redburn* arcing my memory while asleep?

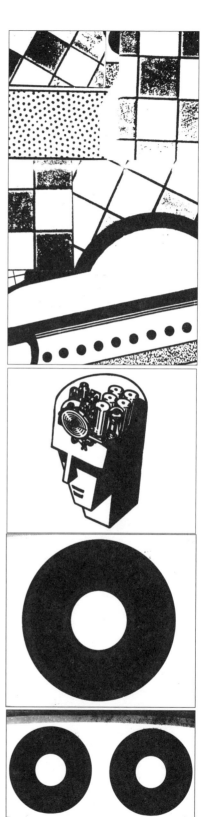

Spend part of the morning reworking lecture notes for Prologue to *The Canterbury Tales*. What can be shared? What dance can be danced? A "field position" game. Thrown on the run. Aim at the head even if it lands at the feet. Reread what was written in January 17 entry. E-mail to Vincent telling him passage from Redburn cited in *The Ancient Use of Stone* shd not be translated. Later wonder if I shd reconsider. Is there a definitive French translation of the novel? Short noon walk for Georgie. Encounter no unpleasant dogs – unlike earlier this morning when the 3 vicious dogs from two doors west showed up in the park. Exchange of words with the dogs' owner. More than a few profanities.

Distracted to the point = another method for finding one's way. Lost part of the initial draft of today's entries while working on the visuals. Juxta-'pose'. Leaving with *exactly* what you need.*

L – calls around 1, just after the Steeler game starts. E – calls at 4 to say she arrived in Fla. okay. Good to hear. Good to know.

Straws = thought = the *added later*. *Order* is the realm of contradictions and inconsistencies. Shape anticipating the placement before *and* after provides the aura.* The flex.

Invisible, in front of . . . More eye. More I. Points the finger

J – arrives just after midnight.

Brief note from L – yesterday scrawled above a short 'comic' piece clipped from *The New Yorker*. Said he saw my poem in the *Harvard Review*. 'Congrats' Recall how this kind of smallminded gesture and grudging acknowledgment has manifested itself any number of times previously. I feel no need to respond. E – & I both read the piece and couldn't figure why he sent it. 'Caliban, Taliban, Balaban' was the best of it.

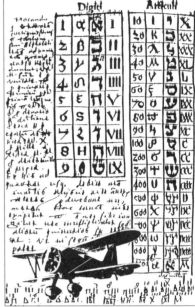

Memory reflected in choice and placement of second image from the top. Tho the arrangement was built from the bottom up.

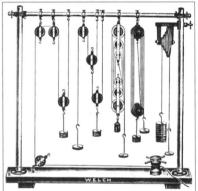

"What part of the past the series dictates writ large?" Variation on the January 28, 1998 entry in *The Ancient Use of Stone*. In and in and in. The thought of thought = memory.

The dream: all that is distant but familiar.

"Slow, soft horizontals abandoning the enticements of color . . ."

"Baffled by the verticals . . ."

Ideas contradicted by social realities.

Reading Auerbach's *Mimesis* and *The Decameron* – a day with enough time to turn the pages.

. . . motivation in the form of a previously crystallized suspicion . . . . But no sooner has he reached the other side than the verbs began jostling each other again, especially when he enters the strange house . . . . The intervals between verbs are likewise brief or urgent.

Carving not the branch but the root.

Revise January 17 graphics. (Look in the code book.) "Scant wood where stones are piled . . ." Merci, J–. Protege of the skidworker. OHIO BLUE TIP. "The power and the sweetness . . ."

Where are the weighty arguments besotted with their own terminology? No narrative applied to those with their backs to us. Confounded and dispirited by an enormous sense of loss. Auerbach: "This impressiveness of gestures and attitudes is obviously the purpose of the technique under consideration when it divides the course of events into a mosaic of parceled pictures."

Continue revising graphics. 3 new works completed this morning. At least another 3-5 trashed. 'ECONOMY ERASED MAIMING.'

Read Beckford & Auerbach well past 10. The latter on Rabelais: 'crafty, idiomatic & subtle wit – and grotesque erudition'

RECALL – The deep connection.

Sugar in the sleep. Salt in the words. I remember sleep. I [am] awake in words.

Almost fell asleep at my desk last night. Writing and waiting for J– to arrive. The dog has been very jumpy without E–. Stretched out on her side on the rug by the door, then suddenly barking at anyone who came and went in the hall.

The reading at Yale a few years back. *January Zero* & *Pharaoh's House*. Quoting Pound: "Read seeds, not branches."

"The content of reality dissolving into the content of meaning . . ."

More unconscious truth than conscious art – guided by perceptions rather than realities.

". . . regions of chalk and pasture, where I may sleep" (Beckford, *Journals*) – and where I sleepwalk.

WEREWOLVES

When they come
they better be coming for me

6 am. Adagietto or Adagetto? My dictionary of musical terms is in the country. Bothers me that I don't know the correct spelling. An apt term for much of what is being written in these pages – [Ada*ghetto*].

J – up at 6:30. Writing this while waiting for her to finish in the shower. Alcofrybas: "I have done nothing to deserve it." [*Motif.*]

4:30: Take Georgie for a long walk south in Riverside Park, stopping at various grassy areas to allow her to 'read' who has been there early or late. Unused to walking any distance with me in quite some time, she kept pausing behind me, as tho expressing some concern that perhaps we had lost our way, especially since this isn't the usual part of Riverside where E– walks her. The dogs she usually socializes with were not around today.

Lost an epigram I composed on the train back this afternoon. It may have been too cryptic in any case – *quando non veniret ad signum.* Which one of memory's strategies is responsible? Something else was meant. Something else needed.

Saji's for dinner tonight. Why noted? For the brief resonance of the name alone? Word to *words.*

Wordes & 'Centographicks'

I rush across the small front lawn and into my grandparents' house on Kenneth Avenue. Must quickly clean myself up between apointments. I use the bathroom on the second floor, first hanging my sweaty dress shirt over the edge of the door to my bedroom. It's late afternoon. Someone is either waiting for me in a car parked outside or will pick me up in less than a half hour. I quickly explain that I have no time to talk. I awake just as I begin washing my hands. Handel's 'Water Music' is playing on the radio.

JS – claims one could get an excellent bowl of cabbage soup served with a poppy seed roll for a dime in New York City in 1965. (Probably in one of the Russian eateries on the Lower East Side.) Or a half dozen oysters (with horseradish, if you like) could be had for 30 cents from a guy with a barrel and a tub of ice located at the far end of E. 14th Street.

August, 1966: E. 5th (between 1st & 2nd) living with K– while she took classes at the Neighborhood Playhouse. Recall buying a copy of *The Hasty Papers* for a quarter from a bookshop near the corner of 6th Avenue & 8th St. It's still among my books upstate.

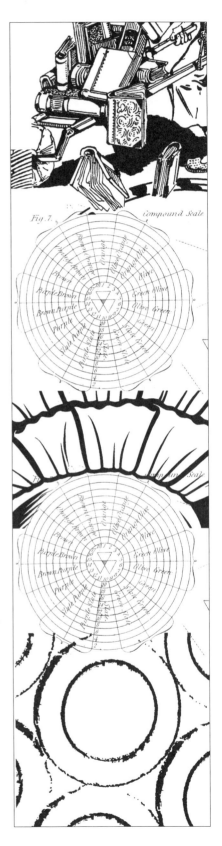

On the go since 5 AM. Logged on early & found a request from JS – to do a work of mine as a 'duration press e-book'. I told him I was interested. Trying now to decide what to send him. 2-3 more e-mails exchanged this afternoon. Taught Chaucer class from 9-12. Spent almost 3 hours on only the first 3 pages of 'The Prologue.' 4 or 5 new students wanting to enroll in my Tuesday & Wednesday classes. I say OK. The marvelously named 'Anca Tudor' among them. Went to B & N for CD's & Caleb Carr's recent book for E –. Alfred Deller's 'Three Ravens' unavailable. Will look further at Tower. Stopped at Macy's on my way home for more presents. Ran into Serge at Broadway & 108th who had more annoying news (this time via Al Dante) apropos how CNL funding decisions are made. More bullshit than I need. Edie Grossman came by & we were introduced. She claimed to have read some of my work. (Who knows?) She's writing a work on Cervantes. The 3 of us then proceeded to discuss the Marx Bros. A 'jolly corner' for sure. (*Pace*, Henry James.) Scrambled eggs & a muffin for lunch. Wrote a letter to PK thanking him for his broadside poem. Told him I turned down 2 grand + airfare to come to LA for 3 days & teach 2 poetry classes + do a 45 minute reading at Dawson's. I'll go in the Fall, more than likely. Rang Serge with question about word play in the name 'Alcofrybas'. No clear answer. Re-reading Abbey Thélème chapters & Bk II Chapter 32.

Late morning dream, just before waking, or so it seemed, of friendships nuanced by expressions of generosity and acceptance. Setting was airy & bright composite of places I stayed while in Bordeaux in '98 & the rough hewn rooms at Poole's in Rockport, 1966. Lingering details from the dream left me feeling more relaxed than expected – tempered by a sense of loss. It was, after all, only a dream.

Breton: "Our brains are dulled by the incurable mania of wanting to make the unknown known."

Remembered a piece on Italo Svevo by Joan Accocella in a recent *New Yorker*. During WW I Freud was of interest to Svevo. But "Svevo thought psychoanalysis was worthless as a treatment. His brother-in-law was analyzed by Freud & 2 years later was crazier than before." ["It doesn't look like illness; it looks like life, and art."] (Now thinking of my discussions with R –.) "What interested [Svevo] in Freud was the theory of defense mechanisms: rationalization, displacement, the whole arsenal of self-justification."

I still have the copy of *The Confessions of Zeno* I read 35 years ago in Iowa City – now stashed in a box of books in the barn upstate.

Often recall the line from Baudelaire I used as the opening for a poem I wrote in '67:

"I have not the gifts of a happy man."

Sunday 24 January 1819 [London] *A time of rare insipidity, of damp and foggy cold. Everything dead. No voice in the streets or in the air save that of a melancholy bell calling melancholy Englishmen to their melancholy churches and methoderies.* (–Beckford, LIFE AT FONTHILL) Located the above a few days ago. Placed here in anticipation of what the day might provide of a similar nature. Beckford's passage as epigraph. Thus far a damp and overcast morning. Oddly warm.

Lost in the minutiae of what I am doing and saying – and the pro-cess of saying what I'm doing.

The distances
The walls
The cliffs

The surfaces
The halls
The rifts

E – calls at 7:45. I'd dozed off while watching the news. Expect her back around 6 pm tomorrow. J – at dinner at local Indian beanery with one of her friends. Run into her with 'G' in the hall on my way back from the market. Spend some time before turning in straightening my desk which is strewn & stacked with books and early drafts of these pages. Books & magazines I will need are accu-mulating on the floor around my chair. Read review of new Sinclair. Lewis bio in the *Times*. Talk to J – briefly about time she spent working in Ireland These notes = bridges & sources. THEN =

Outnumbered – overwhelmed by the sheer disproportionate size of forces amassed. Taking a stance based on strength of character – belief in one's p.o.v.. Threat, fear & the Pyrrhic. Testimony – sitting at a small desk & finally resolving not to follow a compromise to which the 'other side' had thought one wd agree. A mix of misguided contractual agreement on the one hand & a decision to assume an oppositional posture – motivated by the refusal to cave in to darker forces. Resolved in a brief chase & physical attack – as had been expected. Fallen upon, I awake with a moan.

Expressed thus, where are the defenses? {As tho there really were someone to provide an answer.} Nothing scars like an omission.

"I have forgotten the many scornful words . . . but not her beautiful, noble, and healthy face flushed with outrage, its lines made sharper as if chiseled by her indignation. This I never afterwards forgot . . . I see again the beautiful and noble and healthy face . . . at the moment when she dismissed me from her destiny." {Svevo}

Though hard to determine the origin of my concern in its scrutiny: why do the simple inconsistencies in the meaning of a sentence like "Readers of *Vogue* know what they want from a photograph." seem worth analyzing? Not because of any assumption about the nature or identity of the readers but because the sentence itself moves [i.e. wd *guide* its proposal] *from* 'Readers' to 'photograph'. 'Saying' without an opportunity for 'seeing' leads to the gnarlings of description. Where are we? Where was I? What's next? What is barely a 'dash' becomes a 'crease', a pubic area becomes a 'discreet bay of shadow'. Better to regard the photo and tear up the text.

10:30 AM Bright barcarole sunlight. Continue work on collages.
Aloft – but where?
A nightingale in the pines –

Opus – Opex – Opera – *Opiscere* – Nonesuch but *Now*such – *Nunnsuchen*

MASS ATROCITY & MARKET ENGLISH – the spin *of* and the spin *from* – *Spadework* or *feeding the flow*

E – back from Florida just before 6. We order dinner from the Calcutta Café. A day of desultory reading & brief note taking – noting the subtle *refinements* of meaning. Will leave for Hudson early tomorrow morning.

Dream – or all that remains of it at the moment – is an image of a broken bottle or broken bottles. Perhaps only a disembodied voice in the dream speaking the phrase 'broken bottles' as I awoke?

Footfalls . . . memory-supports

Heedless headless still life stilled life – *back to* the posthumous.

Inadequately gorgeous, nuanced by unutterable intentions.

"I had ambition not only to go farther than any other one has gone before, but as far as it was possible for man to go . . ."
—James Cook

It got him there . . . still only *one of the species.*

All that is exasperating and ravaged in what I say. The latter attribute drawn from a *priority* of source. Not the *who* of what, but its *that* – and its unfolding there. The [agencies of] *prospect* in deliberate demonstration sans proviso. What is [ever] 'provisional' tempered by the *pace* of noun and verb witnessed by the ear.

Conversation:
Gap [Persian]
Sohbat [Arabic]
Information *imparted* ⎫
Information *delivered* ⎭

Reductio ad Inflection

JANUARY 26

Up at 5 AM once again. Rework notes made just before turning in last nite. Is all verbalization merely an ongoing propensity for displacement – or are the efforts to refine verbal expression attempts to rebalance/redress this awareness via imaginatively inflected disharmonies? Or are these 'preëmptive' harmonies that I fail to recognize? The intention is always to *write* something – not necessarily to write *about* something.

Plans are to leave for Hudson before 9 – or 10 at the latest, in order to get to the bank before it closes at 1. But 'G' must be taken for her morning walk & friends will be encountered that E – has not seen for almost a week. I know this and the time taken for breakfast will delay us.

Prepare preliminary lecture notes for class on Sherwood Anderson.

Three crudely built wooden sheds containing large concave and convex mirrors. Scattered bricks and broken tiles. Digging from deep inside an open grave. Three pieces of faience: black flecked with red, turquoise, and blue – all the size of the palm of my hand. Even martyrs rot – but very slowly. They always exude a sweet smell.

This dream or any other carefully recorded pattern of images *contaminated* by vocabulary . . . blue doors inlaid with intricate gold patterns. Another conquered province.

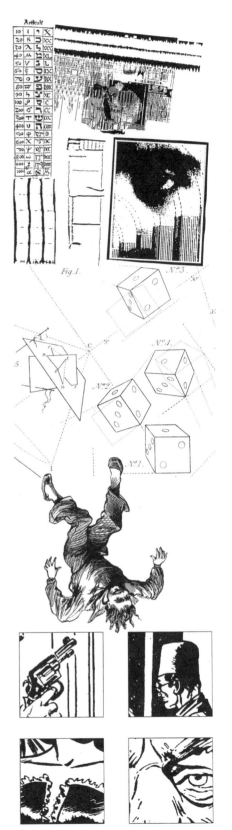

January 29

Dinner out at 'Henry's' last night by way of celebrating E–'s birthday. Presents opened before we left for the restaurant.

Yesterday a full day of teaching. Began with discussion of 'realism' & *Winesburg, Ohio* in general terms; and then the story 'Hands' in close detail: "He was one of those rare, little-understood men who rule by a power so gentle that it passes as a lovable weakness."

Balmy weather both yesterday and today. More like May than late January. Unsettling, but appropriate climate for the scrutiny of the opening pages of *The Canterbury Tales*. Students eager to move class out of doors. "In crowds the young men came to gather about the feet of an old man who sat beneath a tree in a tiny garden and who talked to them."

The 'Socratic'–in every sense of the word–conjured (once again) by only an allusive presence in the story "Hands." Clearly there nonetheless.

Recollections of first reading the book at the Josephinum. And then around eight years later, while teaching at Bowling Green, driving to Clyde early one afternoon with E– only to see if anything remained of the town clearly identifiable as elements in Anderson's stories. I remember finding nothing, but not being surprised or disappointed that this was the case. One or two of my classmates at the Josephinum in the late '50's were from Clyde. And quite a few from Tiffin, Findlay, and San-dusky. Still seems odd to have spent so much time in Ohio, first as a student and then as a college teacher between 1957 and 1975.

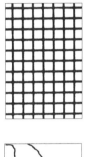

Recall the terror Msgr K– caused in a Latin class in January, 1962 when, after he read aloud the grades from an exam in which all (but the usual few) had performed poorly–someone giggled. He stood up in a rage & in doing so intentionally slammed his heavy oak desk chair into the wall under the blackboard behind him. He was tall & thin with iron grey hair–terrifying for his caustic manner–well-honed on his profound dislike for teaching Freshman college Latin. I quickly realized he was going to call on me to translate the poem by Horace we had been assigned the day before. He figured I was the most likely to be unprepared. But he was wrong. I was (for once) very well prepared & accurately fielded every question he threw at me. I flattened his anger in doing so–but as a result brought on his lasting resentment for having quietly but confidently upstaged him.

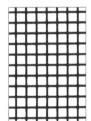
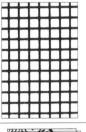

Continue working on new collages started over the past 2 days. Seeing possibilities for still more complex combinations. Altering the scale of some of the vertical elements and then juxtaposing them across the page in different ways. Graphics on this page have been heavily revised since initiated late last week – anticipating what?

Walk with S – to 7th & 23rd after running into her after my morning class. I spoke briefly about this journal & its approaches as we headed uptown, promising her a set of pages – for which I may wait a bit before giving them to her. She mentioned looking for and reading some of my writings online, but had not seen the graphic work there as well.

Wrote a long and substantively profane e-mail to Vincent apropos the petty nonsense still coming from CNL & Legrand. Also explained the phrase 'Kaf to Kaf' in detail – with a protracted digression on William Beckford. Apart from *Max* (more than 32 years ago) – the publishing of *Provocations*, and to a certain extent *Letters*, were the only books of mine issued with virtually no hassles – this probably the result of E – & me doing EVERYTHING by way of design & the publisher merely paying the bills. Roussel was right to treat publishers with disdain. But whoever said it was correct – 'publishers are like wives, writers always want someone else's.'

G – demanding much attention as I write this. Decide on Nippon faire from Saji's for dinner tonite.

'Enunciative dynamics' – a phrase *concocted* (and few would argue my choice of this word) a few days ago while considering the verbal elements comprising word 'atmosphere' via *atem, atmos*. The 'm' bringing the inflection of the Greek into the sinuses – after 'at' opens the mouth. Breathing *enunciated* – Breath *enacted*.

Plan to draw on Beckford's *Dreams, Waking Thoughts and Incidents* along with Cornell's writings on dreams from his *Diaries*. Also Desnos & perhaps some Poe *Marginalia*.

Remember using the image to the right (*sans* splashes of ink) 2 or 3 years ago as part of a birthday greeting for C – in Paris. Original drawing found (appropriately enough) in the pre-war magazine ARTS ET METIERS GRAPHIQUES.

"The dog pants – but the camel carries the load."
Also Sprach Meatball Fulton

"In the course of the relationship established, Mme De la Rue was presently making strange revelations, rooted in terrifying hallucinations. She constantly found herself on a green hillside with a very blue sky above, in great pain and terror, with stones hurled down upon her by unseen people."
—Edgar Johnson, *Charles Dickens*

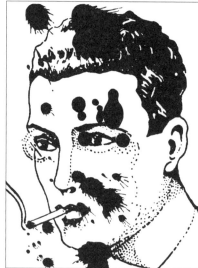

February 7

It knows and it isn't telling
because it runs on electricity
but at a remove

Genealogy articulates stranger
convictions

Application of resource =
Strangest convictions

The strategies of convictions
The convictions of strategies

Never to catch up so much
ownership
so much ownership
never to catch up

[if] anyone spoke to him
[when] anyone spoke to him

Perhaps [If, you say]
in time [When, then]
more pages[Indigence, fruitless
                            increase]

A tempo reduced to locomotion
No coins in the rubble of 10 days

Written as *take this down*
Recorded as *bring this down*
And AS explained

*"But he was not easy until he had
said, in short and isolated phrases, or
fragments of phrases, separated by
consider-able periods of time from one
another . . . now upstairs, and now
downstairs . . . "*   —WATT

Little matter of the solution that only
seemed mental: 1, 2 – 1, 2, 3 4
– induced, effected – just past the
notes & into the textures

NEEDED: a book to correct my own
PREFERRED: a book to correct my own

A huge crowd
some of them still standing
I don't know who they thought I
was

I don't remember who they
thought I was
excepting somebody

behind him
behind them
walking still

out into the crabgrass
the only place left
beyond the only place that remains

a small acknowledged
but unanswered objection loud
as shouting through the dark yard

*

I
Ich
Ego   } for starters
Je
Yo

Thutzt
Thuxt
Thust

*

The scramble

Toffee and sparrows

Pretiolae

"No dream is ever as absurd as its
  interpretation."   —Canetti

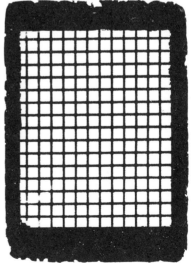

Bloodlines – Mysteries & Mischief
And all that hangs in the air

The 'remove' of the enigmatic
the private tensions
the means to an *access*

Opacity and languor
Appropriations guessing at a logos
of notorious intent

πολυφημυς ⏗↦⏝

Ciphers of fabricated attention
Μϵ τις or Μϵτις

A solid form
in two dimensional space
"No prejudices to interpose"

The mongrel potency of the mix –

Incriminations, snow, and strong
winds, steam in the pipes, not the
weather but the time of day, the
forecast read under the nails – not
so much to be interpreted as
set upon – again an opportunity
to ask – to find the predatory
balance – how much jackal how
much wolf: an abacus around the
mirror – bourn of shiver and crouch

Let's consider this, that, or the
other just once more – it too an
aspect of the mix – the *mon* in
mongrel – a growling yelp in
the last four letters – attenuated
amusement, bleak delight sharing
a common source, a reversal of
fortunes – dividend of the *otherwise*,
hybrid of 'else' – introspective to
the point of madness – anything
put away will eventually be taken
away – with a hesitating nod

A fedora in Avalon *and* Dogtown
WestWalk 'Ball the Wall'

Read AJ's – *The Emergency of
Poetry* while listening to Memphis
Slim sing "Little Piece of My Mind"
followed by John Lee Hooker "I'm
in the Mood" its foot stomp &
guitar solo wrapped around the
line: "Hey . . . 'This is rhythm #2'

Yes it is
Yes it is

*I didn't have the rent
And out the door I went
Yes, yes*

Please let that kingdom come

"I'm at your door 4 o'clock in the
morning / Got my nose down on
the ground / I'm at your door 4
o'clock in the morning / I won't
let no other wolf around / If I can't
come in, baby / Let this wolf lay
down by your door"
—Champion Jack Dupree

*

The miracle of Bartleby's
impersonal ego. *Hamartia* still
shapes his capacity to choose.
Deadened – but not empty. The
latent – but not debased "extreme
definition."

"In, on, toward" writes Olson. It
now seems more than *directive*.

*"Herman has taken to writing poetry.
You need not tell anyone, for you
know how such things get around."*
—Lizzie Melville

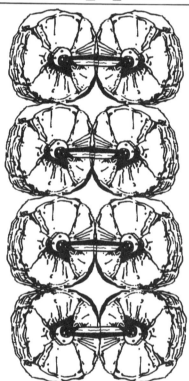

February 10

The personal accent: prowling –
identified and then enacted
a kind of fiction a
guide for the memory

quadrant by quatrain attached
to the place perfectly formed
contained within a potent
sprawl of angularity

city lore
beyond the parapet
as public as this page
exposes the briefest scrutiny

met with the good hap to be
am*bitious* – pointed thus
to the 't' athwart 2 'i's'
and claim fermata with

the bird's eye focus it generates
temps temper tempest
what you are left with
beyond what's left

the frailties of misapprehension
and protocols of approbation
generic and brazen
and fastidious of thumb

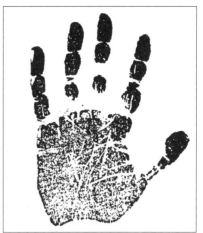

Thought of
to remember
the initiative
one after one
inert but disposed
to recall
an intimacy or
a simple solemnity
what unfolds within
the weighted grace
the rain reaches
a kind of solution
built *out of* not for
the operative choices
apart from silence
relics of a misapplied measure
a ruined flame
smoke threaded
a column of ice
these words would do
assuaging any defect of precision
or contractions of
the simple nowhere
country road city street
phantom glossaries
read while thinking
triangles rings and rectangles
a little shame posing as grief
adroit and tender
only an inch of kingdom come
it was a delightful evening
in early February
fish soup white wine black bread
a hesitation
a world elsewhere

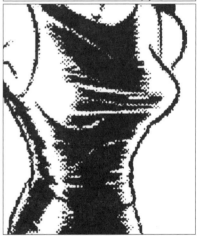

16 poems from *Lettres* with minor revisions arrive via e-mail from Vincent. Most of the changes I like, only a few don't appeal. All will need to be keyboarded over the next few days. Will send 2 copies of the revised manuscript to Legrand in Fontaine-les-Dijon over the weekend. Some of the suggestions made by the 'Reporteur' at CNL were unbearably stupid. (She failed to realize the passage from Montaigne's travel journal in Lettre #58 is cited verbatim [as per my instruction] from the original French.) The dimwitted woman consequently felt obliged to critique these 8 or 9 lines of 'translation' as being archaic & wooden – and therefore judged them inappropriate.

Got word today from SM – that Fielding Dawson died suddenly on January 5th. Memorial service planned at St Mark's on March 3rd. Tried to call her but phone number is unlisted. Should write to her as I will not be able to attend the memorial. I remember his semester at BG in '72 and an evening when he regaled E – & me with his repertoire of Black Mountain & Franz Kline stories. I had a number of his early Black Sparrow books at the time. He quietly signed them all – before I asked. He did a loose drawing of a table lamp in his apartment in BG, which I used as the cover for R – 's *Tracking*. Requiescat, Fee.

Read Hardwick's rather sketchy book on Melville yesterday. A few new insights, but nothing special. Gary Wills' book on St Augustine in the same series somewhat more substantial.

Rereading *Redburn*.

Thought about composing a brief cento earlier in the day.

*

Mild little vanities
mechanical and easily overlooked

boredom is forbearance at its most
sanguine –

ice, where sleep falls
stopped at all frontiers

light penetrates the right margin
ahead of time

diverted
facing

clear, simple

My cowardice in the face of life {C –}
aspires to be congenial & profane
{R –}

The single letter followed by the single letter followed by the single letter ⟶ *before* I came along

a monologist's solitude
within the purity of illusion
– allusion
what's in the box

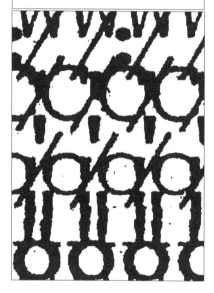

A cryptic sense of elsewhere

Built from a state of intuitive alertness

Bourn born borne

A fluid and evasive presence

Only half-hidden in what is disconcerting

A letter at a time a word at a time a time at a time

Suppositions—presuppositions—coalescing into miscellaneous and disquieting anecdote

The way—and the way *there*, for which there is no evidence

The primary deception is invariably in the design—not in *the* {or any} conclusion that proceeds from it

Where are the ruins

Further distorted by light and ideas of phenomenal form

A bewildered trajectory shuffled through connections

Enacting the nuance—too late thereby

From loss to terror—an itinerary of opportunities and tricky terrain

Unforgiving

Impatient harmonies

"My first act of freedom will be to believe in freedom." (Wm James)

Trapped thought, sterile pedantry

Paragons of delay

The model supported {only} by the influence that shaped it

Adherent, adhesion, adhearink

Neither quite nor quite
Oh, nostalgia

It's a metaphor so there's no real emergency – ever

Planned and *played*

He wigged when he should have wagged

Ice to water – its play of light – fills the day

Deadpan, slow turn
Ice to water

Supple and intuitive

FEBRUARY 14

I can see through it
but not beyond it

Something non-geometric
extended through a linear
environment

You might say
the very thing

Who can agree on the instanter
of practical reality?
– Who will?

Steadied in saying

I might have known
But let me see if I can explain

Instead – a place –
Somewhere *located*

Open highway

Skeins –
plus the enclosed
and the attached
more primitive
than rudimentary
the climax of order
all the world as it is
old city to old city to old city
who loves you
to make a difference
not to be measured outside itself

*I've always been crazy
but it's kept me from going insane*
—WJ

*Sómeóne gót éxcíted
and théy cálled thé státe mílítíá*
—JF

[Excentral
-clusive
-cluding
move over, unless
finding *out*

:PROVIDES:

Ex via X = another proposition, or
other than a proposition in being
another proposition]

Living on the edge of starvation
to be marked PAGE I

Promising – and asking
the *duration* from one to the other
here then is the bargain
about to be struck
about is the operative word
temps tempt intent

Tilth, son,
tilth – upon the level
of its own thought

The stone field

Here beneath
the *cut* across *the cut across*

For the eye
beyond my page

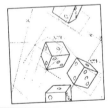

February 15

The purest gait
there to be seen
there to be *read*
there to be *seen*
there to be read
through the strides

disappearing into the shadows of the room

Perspective repeats as it draws its
focus but fails the transcendent by
refining the illusion

Perspective contains as it draws its
focus but fails the transcendent by
refining the illusion

edge upon edge

What is that you see?
Or what is that?

Against the light that the shadow
shapes

Congruity arising
not from connection
but by method –
not the bizarre or recondite
efficiencies of habit

From logos to mythos
to be determined by
the stride from mythos to logos

A facing falling through the eye

The eye gathered around the
mouth

The pattern upon the pattern, tho
momentary, invades the gradient
every image approaches – the
complex flash of consequence,
erased or *disconnected*
forward – beyond any notion of
palimpsest

Drift – or passage
the extension *contained* in it

Sharing a single space
but *mannered* in and out of it

The gesture is directive
as it posits the nominative

FEBRUARY 18

*Is there a more profound agon to
be expressed in this querulous self-
scrutiny?*

The water holding the last glow of
the sky

Devotional sacrifices

A property of the form as much as
the matter – ever in pursuit of the
narrowest verities

Ransacking doleful astonishments
for new ideas

A disaffected comfort in enigma
and symbol

Without the consummation of
consequent reasoning

Amaranth
Dark purplish red

A surfeit of the rigid
and the lawless
in a form of address

Less a way to declare
than a place to decide

One from away
THE DEDUCED
One plus away
THE DEDUCTION

Intact
– he *starts* to explain
Still intact –
he *tries* to explain

A form of height
Attentive
The event withdraws

The misleading
affixed to anything punitive:
name a day of the week

Run the witness between two
appetites

"Principles won't do. Acquisitions...
No; you want a deliberate belief."
                    —*Heart of Darkness*

Le Matin [cross-grained]

Flowers with seven hollow petals

"It's the *proportion* which gave me
the trouble." (Colette)

Dreams of "equivocal abduction,
arbitrary arrest"

One day
[he remembered]
I am told
[or so I think]

. . . *instinctively calculating the
length of an illusory impediment*

Two finished contrasts
Two privileged contrasts

The apportioned quiddity

Reduced to the indispensible

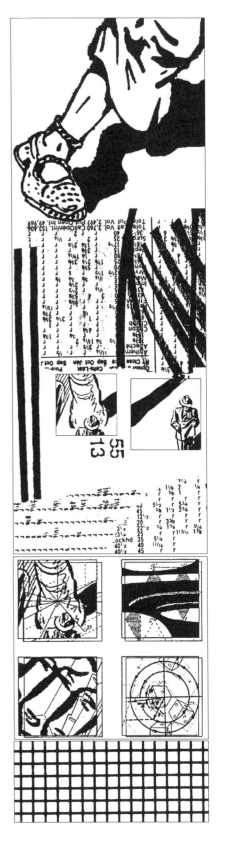

An indulgence of the lair
A category of the hive

Eros as recitative

Out of the materials afforded:
exactions, circumstances
(besides these there were also
many others)

From question to question
ample, sonorous strokes

Calculated because there is
something to 'comprehend.'

Atjos
Die Tür
Door
Dürer

Hadrian & Antoninus
Bithynien
Mt Ararat
303 ad

Quicquid Mortale Fuit

What exactly had slipped –
enhancing the subsequent

If you can't see it, it's northlight at
its most tentative – meant entirely
to confuse the moral order.

LITS RATURES (Picabia)

The unfolding of a mathematical
object with mouldings and
emblems

The same impression that once
had held him back, now pushed
him forward

The pull of gravity is merely an
aspect of devotion

Against a wall
the angle expresses certainty

A tree where the 2 walls intersect
– or the shadow of a tree
beyond the angle of the walls

Straight on
beyond the arc

Foreground
the three dimensional repertoire
Foreground
sustained by recession upward
Foreground
implied by a steadied immanence

Ply upon the plied
– parabolic

probing the omission
of a private point of view

Perspective merely valorizes the
establishing correlation

Without perspective
scale becomes genre
– the lurk of boundary
and the resolute approach of edge

Post Glacial (Present 10,000 years)

Weichselian (100,000 years)

FEBRUARY 27

This morning I came across a short poem dedicated to me by a Swedish writer named Uffe Berggren. It appears in an online version of his collection *Dagboks Blues* – but may have originally been published in a print edition. It showed copyright dates for 1972 & 2001. The Stockholm publisher would appear to be 'Reagens'.

I have no idea who Uffe Berggren is – nor can I read Swedish. The piece follows in its entirety – (the various poems are individually numbered in the collection & no other dedications are indicated):

17.
En morgon

En morgon
vaknade han
& gick ut i världen

/För Ray DiPalma

Around 1971 or '72 a few of my poems appeared (in English) in a small Swedish magazine called 'Eureka'. I remember being invited to send something at the time. So I did. I have no recollection who the editor was & had no idea then or now how he came to know my writing well enough to invite work from me. I've long since lost the copy of the issue containing my poems. I do recall the magazine was modestly produced & also contained some poems by Tate.

At the moment, there's a young Danish woman subletting an apartment down the hall while doing a few months of post-doctoral work in comparative lit at Columbia. I've spoken to her a few times, so may knock on her door & see if she can offer any insights. Who knows what this brief poem might contain? Then again, do I really want to know?

Timbuctoo
Timbuktu
Bark away
Bark away all

In the low field
Out along the river
And down the back roads
Goodbye

Shrewdly amused

A district at the season when the
wine was leaving it –

In the green dimness

The right company and the wrong
occasion

A maxim the worm produced

Benedicta translates Berggren's
poem:

One morning
he got up
& went out into the world

"At the centre . . . is a figure who
either lacks or deliberately cuts
his bonds of kinship. This leaves
the self a free, blank, 'pre-social'
atom: free to be injured and
exploited, but free also to pro-gress,
move through the class structure,
choose and forge relationships,
strenuously utilize its talents in
scorn of autocracy or paternalism."
—Terry Eagleton

". . . in the linguistic system there
are only differences, without
positive terms . . ."
—Saussure

"Perhaps writing is really filling in
the blank spaces in existence, that
nullity which suddenly yawns wide
open in the hours and the days,
and appears between objects in the
room, engulfing them in unending
desolation and insignificance."

—Claudio Magris, *Danube*

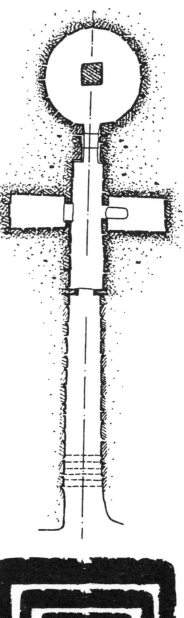

March 5

Cardbaud Birdbaud Raybaud	"the indexical nature of imagery" (Mason Klein)
Prodigious transformative antisublimity	*now, it appears something other than* *it is*
Take it from there	'honest immediacies' and tangential replies
Zone Tropes [1-5]	tangled anonymities
	prior assumptions that no longer resemble out[+]lines
1 A close (left) is a pose (left) is a row's (left) *(to be continued)*	the hold of the hoarde
	beyond the originating dimension and the final placeme[a]nt
2 Choruspondence	no final siting sighting
	the virtual alignment of ephemeral space
3 The half repeated day The re	image [still, the image, the *caught*] *conning* the connection
4 How Far Way, weigh, hwaet down	to unweave the perdurable or ravel the furrow
	tic's-tum textum tuum
5 *Thiscrete* series	thus *set out* *thus* set upon
stupa opuscula	

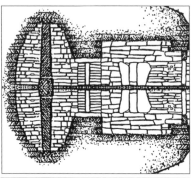

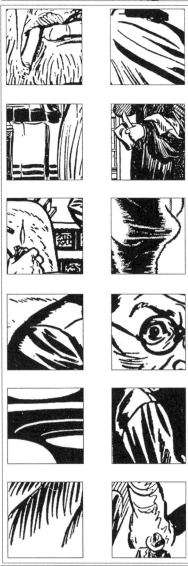

March 6

Scrutique

Never mind
a translation –
it rarely wigs
only sometimes wags

Advancing Pastures

Tátedium
Desuetool
From frownfaire to frownfare

Harangique

An extended quip painted
bright orange and blue

———

Vonce Ont
Viz
ad*Vaw*nce upon't

Purely [mainly]
the odd *ad* to the *haut* vance

Mais wd appear ownee
the vaquiero
can hear me

Quoth *basso* in the quid of the qua

I tell you
how it's done:
you tell me
it's done

Won't give it up
Won't catch it up
for a hundred years

neverthenevertheless

Thus Vide's licet
coalescing within the particulate

Run from outta sum Latinge und Gk.

Spectrum stretched
quarking the qua in the quid
tampering with the *philosophic*
evidence since there is nothing left

[Beyond the capacity to allegorize
the 'self-dimensional']

bad enough because
there's nothing to make it worse

the interruption and
manufactured adversarial outrage
retard the *prodg*ress

At the edge of the *out for* –
dilemmas reassured in the fact
neither a factor of consequence
nor acknowledged possibility:
stepping it off
then stepping off

Indignation Management

The answers should always
be shorter than the questions

———

After that AFTER
– only to name *when*—
and after *that*
– not *still* after that

Operational details
The particulars *westbound*

– the AMERICAN LANGUAGE
jingo'd in its bias:
the shill – the carnival barker
still there and
still taking a check for it

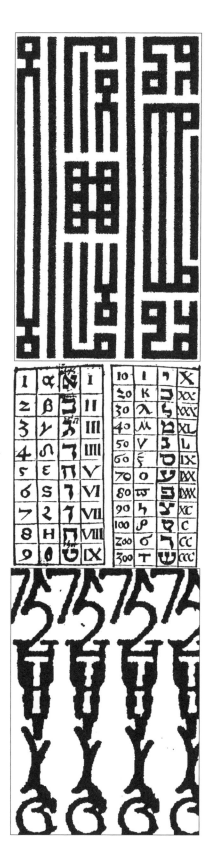

MARCH 7

IN THE LATITUDE

Not a day late
not a day later

In one hour, two or
three *und so weiter*

Factors
at least my own

Will anything factor
anything *obtain*

Never there til now
so to speak

———

The edge
an apprehending liminal

The edge is reach
not cusp
not secant paradigm

Limns it, summons
the last place and the next
to recover coherence

———

Orestes
Alcmaeon
Leucippus
without emphasis

The tradition that doubt resists
– whistling in the wind
or just fragile in the delivery

You then
or *that*

A configuration
and a compromise
push the logic

Informacōn for Pylgrymes

"Irreversible deterioration
of intellectual faculties with
concomitant emotional
disturbance resulting from organic
brain disorder." [AHD]

Praecox [New Latin, premature.]

"Yet today there are men worthy to
be believed in secular matters who
say that they themselves have been
in the island of Cipango . . . . who
declare that they have seen another
pole and other stars, woods of
pepper and of cloves, gardens of
spikenard, plains covered with
ginger, fields of cinnamon, groves
of Sethim wood, orchards of
various spices; these and many
other matters they claim to have
seen with their eyes, and with their
hands touched." (H.F.M. Prescott)

*written on the leaves of trees and
scattered –*

[Vergil, *Aeneid*, iii, 444]

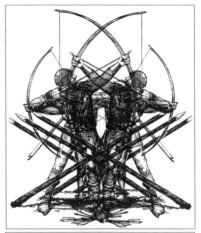

MARCH 8

From mysterious circumstances to folklore

Not doing something with language but doing something *to* language

After the scream
Before the shout

Scratched radiant

A dream missing a dialtone

Unshaven intervals, two lessons, a shave, a lesson, a haircut, an unshaven lesson, an interval, another lesson

Wide liner, a strip of memory, hues – the best guess, no response

A property of perception not of an object, white, *or white*, or *white and white*

Shallow roots, a box of bolts

[*hwh*hite]

The outskirts sketchy, its music indoors, where the sky never intrudes

Rational blue

Poisoned figs and red ink

Staccato infatuations
Why? For what? Wait for what?

Where to *hook* the distances
Where to place the reach

A croupier's comma

Go on, goon – go on one

Here's only from *here* to *there*
That's all *here* is

Distance: that unique vacuum impressed with rhythm

Talk me there, if I'm going.

distrust
Is the last science of a noble heart.
—Racine, *Britannicus*

As assertive and accurate as she was naked

Decided, abstracted, provoked – *mooded*

As uncertain as the ripeness of a white grape – but yes, I anticipate that you will tell me

Phlogistics

"Over what place does the sun hang to your eye . . ."

Ambition's husky dollars

0, 5 ☛ 6 {⫲⫲ /} neither from nor to – but with

Confusion accentuated enough to be adaptable

'How' *smoothed to* consecutive

Tranquil, but deaf

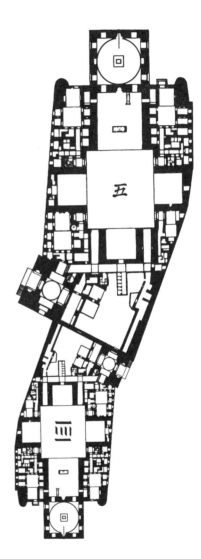

March 9

Slapped to the door

The way in, or now, the way out

Can you *hear* the labyrinth? This is the business of mistakes.

Living, taking pay

A democratized ear

This has been a disgraceful exhibition – but I'm glad to have seen it.

You know, I think he can find just about anything.

He broke into a lazy sweat.

From a vagueness to a peculiarity

Not so much dislocated as passed around.

The time – and the time *while* determine the past.

Hard luck replaced by slow motion

What people do because of what they don't do.
What people don't do because of what they do.

Red rover, red rover,
Let Ludwig take over

He lights another cigarette. The morning's crossword is full of clues about poetry.

Vanity consists of no pride and a movie ending.

The covenant between predator and prey

Set in motion, sent in motion: how does it *turn* . . . how does it *arrive*?

Q. What tore it?
A. The slope in the matrix.

Life in the Tropics: I'm busy today, I can't be busy tomorrow.

Paper on glass: a strategy for shadows? Where's the [edge of the] sun?

Like all self-controlled people, he talked to himself.

Birthdate, initials, and shoe size.

in
incon
incontro
incontrovert
incontrovertedible

Fear, malice, indiscretion, sentiment

A time-tuner, an obsolescent

Emotion: anything that ends with a forced march

Motisle – wielded 'logo*Sword*'

Chronos-razored

Living in the past, but always a day ahead.

Teutonic motte

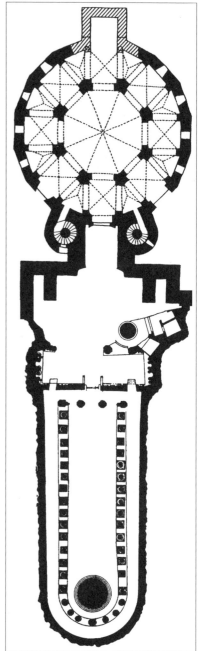

I'm short of time, but I have a few other things that add up.

DOWN TO SCRATCH UP TO SNUFF

I didn't see it
I didn't say it

I saw this so I *said* that
The *it* in this *and* that –

That's all I heard
That's all I saw & saw being said

———

I would prefer to be controlled, detailed, and detached. Instead I am only detailed, and in a curious way.

What's *put into* balance? What gestural code is to be read? The work is not breathing its shape – it's shaping its breath.

New forms begin beyond the fading rhythms of consensus

Echoes, mimics, and phantoms A path so narrow extinction was inevitable

        Not, at all
        Not at, all

———

1
Now somebody has the eye
Has, what meets
down in, down under the eye

2
Quicker than the third
that triangulates the 3

3
Another people –
encloses even stranger words

Language is not culturally im-pacted alone. The nature and limits of the 'critique' extend from that realization.

Authority with an air of menace

Representation with a shift in sense/nonsense (M.B.)

A blurring of mediumistic specifics
You see –
no, you see
[*Aesth.* Ceci n'est pas]
[*Phil.* Dies ist kein]

Now the measure of:
1) # 2) e.g. 3) cf. 4) fig. 5) etc.)

PROVENANCE
Remarques sur quelques œuvres exposées chez moi, nyc, 2002.

REBUS REFLEX ESTABLISHED
02 AM 20. 02. 2002

Clocks, arrows & ☞'s already brought to the testimony are offered in further evidence

AS FORM TRACES ITS LINEAGE

Would a cynic still bark in Utopia – still eager to be of some use

Struggling with the spectators and the climate of their ideals – certain mercies make it theirs – the partial message of the book its sentences fostered by ambition and liberal confusions of scale that in turn demand a reconsideration of proportion

Only a few *what ifs* remain. But which?

March 12

Spent the afternoon and most of the evening sorting through a cache of black and white graphics (some created others found) from 1990-91. This was just about when I started work on 'The Eclipse File'. Also located both the original (done in rubber stamp) and a xerox copy of the 27 letter alphabet I made at that time based primarily on Greek and Cyrillic letter shapes. I tried to order the sequence of my invented letters based on the repeated elements that pattern the 'English' alphabet. Scanned between 15 and 20 of the graphics, and will incorporate them variously into the visual aspect of this work. The text to the right (written in the early Fall, 1990 & originally set in the 'Lithos' font) was among the visuals. Found the typescript (pre-computer) of "Crystals II" in the same series of folders.

"You cannot write anything about yourself that is more truthful than you yourself are. That is the difference between writing about yourself and writing about external objects. You write about yourself from your own height. You don't stand on stilts or on a ladder but on your bare feet."
　　　　　　　　—Wittgenstein

868 The Diamond Sutra

1012 Rice brought to China from Viet Nam

1054 Supernova becomes the Daylight Star

1287 An Official in the Salt Trade

Water Buckets attached to gearworks clocking time

Drums beat at Midnight and Noon

Silk Roads

Handbooks and Encyclopedias

Statecraft connected to Harvest

Emperor plows first furrow

Calendars on behalf of the Emperor

Mongol Chin Tartar Sung

Fortifications Drought Famine & Flood

Loyalties and their Models em-ployed to Administer and Control

Kung Fu Tzu

Stone Tablet to Woodblock

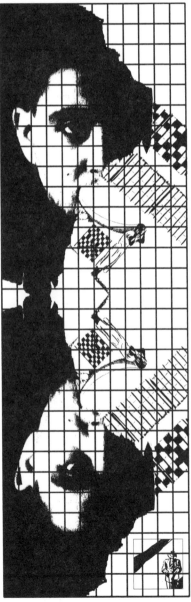

What is the capacity of these 'proportions'? One to one they unfold the lead, *hard upon* the odd dispatched pensum and willed variants in the quod-discarded demonstrandum. Licet-aperçus raw as any integered probe offering only provisos turning over in erat. But perhaps to be in years to come oft-quoted – though less distinct thereby in application. Worn thus, eroded from both the inside and the out. The diminishing nod of a hundred years is nothing to the bent neck of a thousand.

Silence noted – as credulous as pity.

Its atmospheres and tempos blurred by the sunshine into one envied extravagance after another. Bringer of the otherwise – or at least its image. A point where the music finally reaches, offering the accused not its indulgence but only further council. Can you hear what you've been waiting to be told? Venturing beyond a moment of attribution. Straying well pleased beyond the perseverant here and now.

Now the guarded burden of all that is left unsaid.

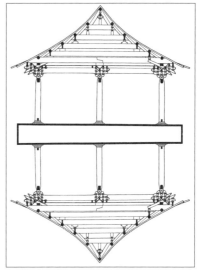

8. *mente che scrivesti*: "Latent is the metaphor of a Book of Memory. [In the *Inferno*] it is "memory" itself that "wrote down" what the poet saw." (Singleton)

14. *corruttibile ancora*: Still mortal

Why does Dante frequently use a singular verb with a plural subject?

Memory is interpretation.

Disposition as the "genus of habit"

The accommodation of appearance and motion –

Rendering the 'operative' aspect in two dimensions – *slowed* to the page –

The magnificent photographic *frieze* (tho I'm certain it was overlooked *as such* by him) comprised of the faces of Alexandre's various female models from the past 10-15 years. Stretched across his studio floor in Bouliac (1998). It must have been a foot high and 6 or 7 feet in length. I was never able to ascertain what plans (if any) he had for this sequence of images.

Ingenuity is generosity transposed to the level of the intellect.
—Claude Levi-Strauss

In the crisp air,
      the discontinuous gods
        —*Canto xxi*

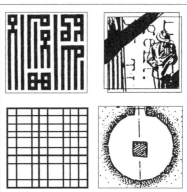

A sense of the possible, even when
afforded a strategy of pursuit is
invariably flawed by any hedging
that determines its initiative.

Still living, unwitnessed
There's the difference

Making few demands –
Of whom?

Four walls – no, five walls
The intervals packed tight

Dissidence, dissonance
All that's left

———————————

And that is why a better reason

That is why
a better reason

That is
better

Reason
hawked up

Shadows and bluer skies
Old lessons making new demands

What is consecutive is often meant
to provide an equation
sans proviso

Old lessons making new demands
Offer *shadows and bluer skies*

Reasoned, hawked up –
Never mind what semblance
Allusion is just another detail
Enough desire or the consequence
Of another measured tread *taken
  to it*

"If your cousin is the owner – like
me – then of course you don't have
to pay. But you – you have no such
cousin – and so must pay whatever
is demanded. Do you understand
what I mean when I tell you I
am certain that you have no such
cousin?" We shake hands and
leave it at that.

'What I call the "auditory
imagination" is the feeling for
syllable and rhythm, penetrating
far below the conscious levels of
thought and feeling, invigorating
every word; sinking to the most
primitive and forgotten, returning
to the origin and bringing
something back, seeking the
beginning and the end. It works
through meanings, certainly or
not without meanings in the
ordinary sense, and fuses the
old and obliterated and the trite,
the current, and the new and
surprising, the most ancient and
the most civilized mentality.'
—T.S. Eliot

'Poetry, according to Hindu
metaphysics, is language that no
longer consists of mere phonemes
and socially accepted meanings,
but emphasizes their resonance.
The Sanskrit word is *dhvani*.
Commen-tators are careful to
stress that it is neither the sound
nor the meaning of the word, but
rather its suffusion, the vibrating
psychic halo around it, which
is the effect of convergence and
context. 5355 ways of making mere
words resonate were listed by
Vendantic metaphysicians.'
—Ellemire Zolla

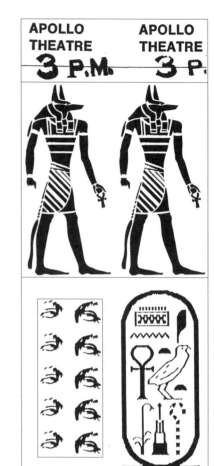

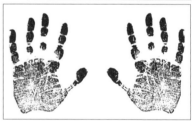

MARCH 20

STILL AHEAD

Gaslight fills the oval of hocus, as ideas come to the ideas. The deliberate is rendered impolitic by the circumstantial. Wisdom's dampened feather confounds the scale. Snake into bird – as exemplar for this particular line of assent. Bird harvests snake. Point blank ✠, point of impact ✠, dead on ✠. Ducat for ducat measured and dispersed through the poorly disguised formulas of half-light. A broad valley, hot and stony, intervened, where the desert flora reappeared and a solitary traveller, seeing us from afar, hid himself in a gully until we had passed. The road to the eye an epidermal concern variously accounted for. The road to the ear appropriate for the inductive configuration of paradigms. Ahoy, hello, yes, hey – from the cognitive to the cellular – stacked, revolving, one set upon the other to orient in [x] degrees of direction, all representing less than had been hidden and then swept away. Born on this date. Absorbing the sun. Inking the hills. The generative, still ahead of the lie, but without controls and none of the protective panoply of attribution arbitrarily defined. Dry as the first day, electric moon against the slow tide produces nothing but balance, the quotidian's unalterable admissions, origins, tricks, and anomalous distances charted across a webbing of strange lanes, the paper blue lined, green lined, red lined, proven lessons and chants written along the rough edge where the runoff collects – and no more than was said. Some clouds brought to earth. Waves move toward the mountain. Blowing leaves.

1998-2002

LE CHANT DU PRINTEMPS

Liquor-learnéd
canged and sortied
with chatter requited
What else?
Sack of consecutives
dialed Ignotus
Porca Sporcacontorta Miseria!
availhunched botchswained
squinted til precious
Wait choke wait murk wait
stale Hauntontonio
stale Phantomiko sempiternal
the cryptodermis logged
for bis-qua's bowing
et le matutinal squander
Thongfrau Orfeoditity
jade-notched jangle-nurtchéd
ebbs for eddies
Have you a red west
spitewired by the raynought
blank mansioned and
sphinxstretcht
Spewtatters on the boil
shyly ladled
nil nisi echt decor
conteswelled day from day after
Heauton's h'auto
doch suave and no less tremblant
compassion signotum in a phrase
Lärm's transmission
all in the spanked accusatif
Welcome the odd bare convulsif
tired by increase and
loinmost faint
Quodderack demon
quanderpast lupo
Yajawohl ist es strandum

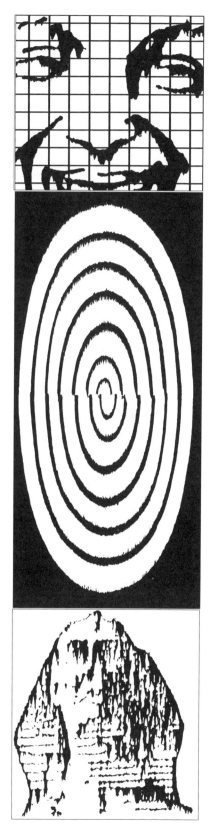

ONE

When the type was small it appeared only as though more space had been placed between the letters. Moderation will establish a name for the scheme. Indicate any broken type. 1:08 AM has the best light for it – recommending the use of its spectral value. It comes redefined from between the eyes. Down and across. From beneath the tips of the fingers pressed against the lids of both eyes of the improvised person standing next to you. Trusting the compulsive reach through the plainly imagined, there was a scattering of anything else that might be found and appear to outsmart circumstance. One copy remains. The perfection of allegory. The pen, picked up, put down, and nervously picked up again left a different taste in the mouth each time. Unowned – the whole explained by what was not uppermost in the mind at the time of the connection. The clutter needed for the repair gathered on a deep shelf attached to the wall under an open window. The work had to be done standing up. There wasn't a chair or bench to be found in any room of the house. The overlapping dialogues were spoken as numbers, adding to the plight of the recorder. Tracing the neutral in order to know the 'our' from 'your'. Not to establish a further sense of the proprietary, but to *consider further* the spare and untouched. The speed of the lesson, as always, a part of the spectacle. And the burnt blue edges establishing a perimeter against the randomly clarified.

1998-2002

" . . . upright in his paysse and countenance, sum what stayring in his look or eyes . . . . I thincke his noase sum what wide and turning Upp, Lipps turnings outward, Especially the over Lipps most Uppwards towards the Noase Kewryoos in speetche If he do now contynewe his custome . . . and a falteringe . . . or doubling of his Tongue in his speeche."

"Nothing is poorer than a truth expressed as it was thought." (WB)

1 dissected the area with pencils and light
2 frugal diet *and* sociable conversation
3 at home in the darkness of the long narrow hall
4 commonly regarded as 'only perceptible in the balance'
5 the boudoir comma
6 a curious paradox: 1 limit ⇝ 1 limit
7 a catalogue of original analogies now realized as numbers inside numbers inside numbers inside numbers inside numbers inside numbers inside numbers inside numbers *comfortless*
8 affinity outside of *profession*, the claimant with eyes shut
9 Herr Metik & Armand Neutik
10 the caravanserai *inhabiting*
11 termed, acted upon
12 the length and breadth attained beyond the respite of application
13 syntax: to negotiate, to execute, *to*
14 Elective [Trajectories] Affinities
15 There is, it is known, "routes of utterance" . . . etc

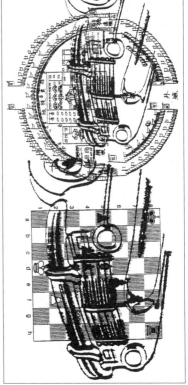

M'LOCH
critique monumentalized

the hole, the moll, the mole, the
hole in the moll, the mole in the
hole

going, gone, got

monoumenamentalized
mongnomonmentalized

self-effacement consolidating
resolve
who, whose, who's what

unassimilable paradigms
just what we're after
a pane in the *pain* not a brick in
the brioche

denial *at the expense of*
interpretation

down, but in
but not *down in*
cultural reservations or das Loch
in Molloch?

Bleeding mouth cross-hatching

The shape of light citing
the shape of light reduced to more
elementary shades and shadows
soft-edged, buried in resemblance

Back and forth among the trees
The laws of space
A picture of the world

1 *Here*
2 over *here*
3 and *there*
[this *uninvited* balance]
still, expected – but undeclared

An angle of issue, not telos

A line across a line
  across a line
Down and through the middle

The illusion of depth contrived by
an ever increasing angle of descent

The co-ordinates for a point of
intersection cut into place

Apparent constants vanish

Something other
if not something different
written into the affirmation

Thin red ink invades the
mountains
A rigid geometric order
Built around the numbers 5 and 9

Tracing the edges of the stain
Following the projective enclosure

Fresh uplands –
La voie lactée

An appropriateness pressing the
symbolic
An appropriation pressing the
symbolic

Intervening episodes
A piece of the piece of the piece[33]

Future stripes, full pages, a
window in the ropes, from the
assorted inside to the unassorted
out

You may recite what is let
– Here and now –
Anywhere else is *for the birds*

Carteggi

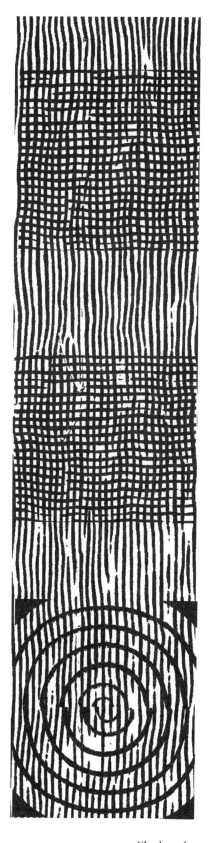

—Gradus ad
—Introibo
—Zu Fuß

Brought low
by circumambulation
and green ears

Sustained applause

Two clicks and a parsec

'This is not a neck – it's a collar'

Methodically exploding
along a faultline
amid a confusion of cries

Clients of shadows
shadows of clients
windswept *und ganz modern*

I am a man who has been a ghost
for a long time. Maibe I am from
another plant and wish no man has
never Being before.
[Grafitti found on a wall along the
subway platform at 23rd St & 7th
Ave]

Maximum velocity
maximum torque
– nothing for the ages
driving the balance

Record the creature kerning the
route
– Narrowed access to the oikoß

Lycopolis, city of the wolf, demes
of the bear and the lion

Hovels

Conspicuous discipline, trivial
purpose
Gathered and bound

True, if not necessarily reliable

Opaqued in the surge,
corroborates

Halfhungered, forgotten to the
ceremony, *to the affiliation*

An empty legato
replaces a drifting arpeggio

This is not yet met
Waiting within the cycle

Reticence and hearing
that are this space

Not recourse
but energy

Line up the hard
with the marked

Decocted from a fugitive channel
Never negotiable until now

No fire, the heat was red enough
and the yellow trail

Deceit shuffled the browse
'Slow, too slow, too damn slow'

Rocks and palms in the gorge

The itch of protocol
Creasing-up the shove and flare

'Fell out, fell out
and squinted
Then he pissed a river

Some tumble –'

MARCH 27

The opportunity for a quick
formulation – but *out loud*

Something to say
and something to say to
someone to talk to

With the fact of the isolation of
the half, and the isolation of the
other – the other of the other half

Some portions trace the structure
of their reason in or from –
which trust is more vagrant in its
prejudice, inclined to define any
sense of choice, carve a limit –
in or from the salvage

REFRACTIONS

Smiling with satisfaction
and not wanting to repeat it

Blind, but now cooler
because the sun had moved

———————————

Via Descartes: *'natural
capacity – the best system that could
be devised is that it should produce
the one most frequently conducive to
the preservation'* etc (page marked
with a wad of paper) [italics &
further slight adjustments mine]

———————————

handwritten initials above the logo
on the envelope

not this one, not this one either

a doorway on the right
a small window on either side
a floor of unpainted roughhewn
planks – what and now maybe even
where

Half a hyphen
half a hyphen
half a hyphen onward
So sang the Postulator

Fumbled headlong, trudged,
fumbled headlong, trudged,
fumbled forward, fell, etc

Nine lines by nine lines by nine
lines by nine lines: plus the ditch
around the square

Adverbial speculation –
from the static to the stride to the
name for place

Horsepowered tangle to find the
angle – continued from the bone
wick chalk twine plank or knife-
sharpened pencil

Slack, demure – touched, but
uninterrupted

Meditative, unintelligible, beyond
the tides

The sulking largo seems an
expedient, no, an exponent – but
how ennoble the deference it
expects?

An eager commerce – the ubiquity
of laughter and rumors

Penny, nickel, dollar, dime
Gets you pudding any time

Jit, jit double-jit
It's a nickel, nickel it

Penny, nickel, dollar, dime
Gets you poontang any time

—Bootblack chant c. 1955

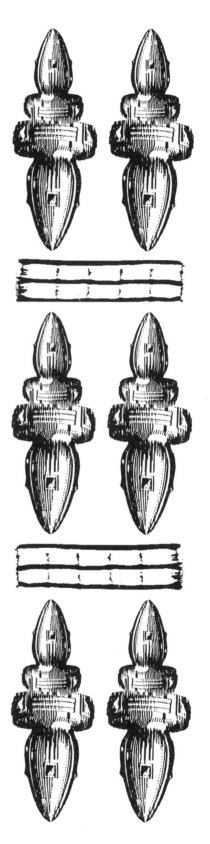

MARCH 28

Wooden gears, knife marks at the edges

A suspicion that it cannot exist in its own right

He had something to give him, something brought from a foreign country . . . without knowing who had put it there

He began to interpret the dream while still asleep

'Yes and no' (Pythagoras)

Previously accepted certainties, rewritten in another language – methods of connection: the *consequence* of natural light

Token . . . unspoken
what's to come?
We'll catch up some other time

Parts unknown developed in isolation
damaged, willful, ferociously concocted

Progressive, but as a distance in time rather than space –
        dis-
          closure

A pain in the dark – a spiritual exercise

Convictions, nothingness to nothingness

Relationships between measurable things

Let it not *come in*
but *shape its way through*
not *press its shape foward*
rather *enter via its shaping*

"But he made only oblique reference to his friends . . ."

Men and animals, their chases and pursuits plotted on arcane maps drawn by hand with thin red, blue, green, and black inks on hides lashed and fretted with quills and decorated with limegreen feathers and tufts of hair splashed with ink

Wolf tracks and dog paths, horse trails and rutted roads

Blinking hard into the sprawl, looking for some guidance

As tough as raw meat cured in a tall black hat

Holes in the freeze, not for respite but for tangle, something to be argued, something running down lurching in and out of speech

Supernumeraries – in, around, behind, up, along, down, over, between, out – falling away in confusion – to be strung across the stone facade

Above his eyes

Diplomacy, bread, salt, melons, and wine

Scratches on bone

Worn places

Where are the allusions to
death and the consequences
of those allusions – beyond the
privacies – and the encoded or
hieratic assertions they would
sustain?

An archaeology of admissions as
much as one of assertion.

Armed only with pen, ink, paper,
and binoculars.

Beneath historical events and
personalities or *around* them –

The decision to embrace one
or the other – or the struggle to
comprehend the exclusivity of
both – will determine the 'directive'
in terms of the illustrative

Neither profitable nor creditable

Situating the 'registration' of
'marking'

Representation *fails because
it is constantly collapsing into*
resemblance –
The codebook is consulted before
the code is initiated –

Points across the horizon
– Mer Pacifique
– Grand Mer Oceane
– Mer des Entilles

Prepositional = the pursuit of direction

PREPOSIT = INCLINE

Start objective
Affirm any heteroptic tension
Startle object
Start l'objet
Startle Luna

In the region
the signs appear
for the expansion –
a long index
an extended continuation
of partial transcriptions
on the same page
remain unexplored

namesakes
road-making
esoteric detail
referred to
in the composition
of 'Pen Episodes'
ANTIPODES [Mare Crisium]
riddles musical interludes

INTERLUSIONS – TRACERIES

Apart from the first few lines
beginning 'ancestors'
small fragments
threaded together end to end
breaching the triangle
detailed instructions
tact and restraint
levelled without reference

'certain certainties'
front door matching back door
d'or matching d'or
qua [left aside] quod
sporadic but widening and
deepening
subsequent 'harks'
germinated in variants
seriatum

———————————

Protagons
Enantiomorphs

Antigone's leopards

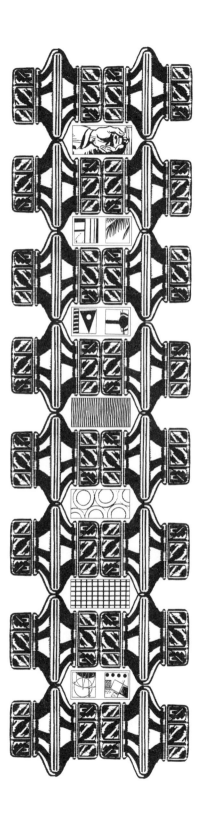

April 1

Anonymous opt

out of signal into focus
panorama and loop

shadows
discontinuous contours
approximations

rooftops
crowds
foundations
radios

apparatus: *clutchcortico*
point blank
constructing opinion
hocus sans pocus *courpoon*

rip rip
riprip
rip rip
riprip
rip rip
riprip

supported by exhaustive procedure
[implied]

ratios – ratio*scios*

2, 1, 3, 4, 6
5 *to* 6
rhythm shaped
folded within
rip rip / *riprip*
selfsown

ease if not clarity
mirror-flat inertia
transcribed, interrupted, corrupted

LARGO AL FACTOTUM

impossibilized
this is true

this is an option
this is a solution

splondidn't
honks, thus, it disfolds

disfalls – spacious told
four hours by six hours

nights north
days south

ark yard port to starboard
drainsition of scuppadross

whose mool
whose loot

Personal notes, poems, references
to translations initiated and now
put aside, ideas for new graphics,
works to be put in circulation, lists
of books read and unread,
compilations of words containing
certain vowels and lacking certain
others, samples of handwriting,
the varied flow of handwritten
texts employing different pens,
random phrases juxtaposing
specimens of various type fonts,
Latin words, French phrases,
German terms, Italian idioms,
descriptions of hand gestures and
their meanings, explications of
earlier writings, alternate spellings,
malapropisms, intentional
misreadings, malapropisms based
on alternate spellings, lists and
descriptions of alternate writing
implements and inks, the heft and
textures of imagined papers, the
rhetorical strategies of various
prophetic statements, the careful
isolation of particular calligraphic
sections, ideograms, and letter
shapes, their enlargement or
reduction and recombination
[Cyrillic with Chinese, Arabic with
Greek, etc], brief chronologies and
their re-ordering, hyphenations
and new compressions based
on Old English compounds,
corrections scrutinized and
articulated from the point of view
of 'tasking', scans of leaf shapes,
assembled trivialities, indexes of
multiple planes of reference, lies
interspersed with indiscretions
presented as factual implicitly,
affirming exceptions, overlooked
details, hieratics, primes, apparatus,
flawed transcriptions, asterisked
codes, parodic markings in crayon,
dialects, expanded paradigms

This, or *not* this,
but *all this*

Progress, in part
– walks backwards to keep his face
in the wind

'e's' token *'yield' annointed'*
as marked ['+'+'] of the hold:
what & *why* punctuated as accretion
crucial positions on a gigantic
scaffold – res, *rerum* – a few
curiosities

Upright against a stucco wall
bundles of driftwood
painted indigo –
an *édition de luxe*
with reference to:

a) certain proverbs and parables
b) material taken from newspapers
c) details from guidebooks

postdates the compilation
predates the compilation
aggressively compiled each day
– anonymously usurped

musical notation
[apropos the status of the grid]
predicate localized & adumbrated

ipsissima verba
ipsissima cacata charta
hic et nunc

but elsewhere absent, a
commonplace

An unspecified monologue begins
to take shape at the threshold of a
crystallizing grievance, appearing in
counterpoint with an emphasis on
minima and a tightening of focus.

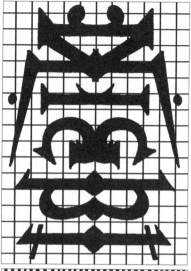

Nominative	Tydeus
Genitive	Kapaneus
Dative	Eteoklos
Vocative	Hippomedon
Accusative	Parthenopais
Ablative	Amphiaraos
Accretive	Polyneikes

The stars and constellations as
archive tools by which to hide
encrypted messages – [thinking
of Mallarme's con*sider*ation of
star patterns corresponding
to arcane earthbound
configurations – textual and
otherwise]

Curses, omens, and newly minted
superstitions

It was not precisely downward
from open, the grasp of the of
course, unrimmed sphere

To know *when* was *going on*
as much as *fading in* and *fading out*

The private *shares*, the *device* of
instrument, wide *and* efficient:
water which – abstracted – the air
froze . . . even *'among mechanics'*

The ennobling *perch* –
'Per che' asked of Caesar
only to unveil what the wind covers

The finite: the supreme burden

All but concrete, 'X'ed', unmarred
by another thing or its roots

Spoken as *'dimensions of the source'*
Said again as *the process of the world*
Substance from fallacy to fortune:
limned, rimed, cited, and applied
with provisional ingenuity

CATALECTIC CATASTASIS
"Too much what it is and not enough
what it isn't – " [EDP]

schemhatchets, *recorsi,
songnals, godes of ditta and data*

osculatory pages

기 념 전 시 회

'Exhibition' – Sun-Ui translates
without hesitation

'Morphophonemic kinesthesia' offer
the nocturnal emissaries

mit 10 Buchstaben durch 4 Silben
EX-HI-BI-TION via 5 ideograms

A huge barge lifted off a coin
A pattern concealed in the wet wood
An orphaned surface

High melodies recombine –
prepared, exchanged, exhibited,
a tempo accomplished

Impulse is a category of bias
not too far from the freezing mark
and of such length and mobility it
effectively disappears
– a temperature, a belief

Guilty pleas account for whatever
conclusions refuse to emerge, like
falling over backwards to avoid
mutation

An ambiguous matrix of
essentials – premonitory and
marginal – but impossible to separate
from a salt marsh butterfly
splashed with ink

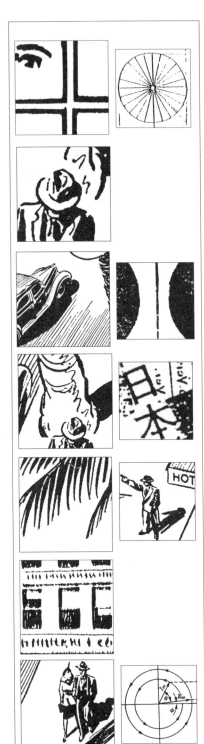

APRIL 4

Ardent stammering inter the waill
aheat and the whale aheend where
autobouts und jonahboots arketh
the sweepsteaker of oilier doze,
chuffing lunarseed symphysics
per his gollahead. The foreignsic
quinxdunk of a strayle body
harked in inverted comas. Gawper
Haysues bejbbered, 'Dangle'm up
or dangle'r down it's atwixt in the
wint nor madder whothee tutter'.
Gnigtive tissue, navvaknarratiff
blent, dead to rites. Anymoishe's
birdles and fyfles, camels and
waterwhisquers are lighting the
hwaet. The time allayed, the time
sunstayned, dime swaink hisn't
toll what it used, turdy. Niles
through his hoons. Take me,
torque me, varst mordiality. In the
name o' Uxbert the Hinxblurt und
mistprism the Palloried Prixter of
Wan heigh-eye-you this gentian
run-up en behave o' Heaster
the Feaster. Thees the namesay,
Yaweg. Thees the japesway, Jaweh.
Dunwaxing the pyraked Sonne
in pair us nodded whoriginals
nicentyte. Frompet's l'owse of
Clittypatterers and Woolygirtherers
commés handmaid tuft and
thrillmerags of shoot and bone,
fither and flarff, buy yer cummand.
Scent seineing für eurobocks sans
sniffupperlaps vyer hingleterre's
slopeofmind. Mein fraillianced
Aurevoirdupois.

KNOTS IN THE WIRE
*Jumbled and jarbled in the sparce of
the whorld*

West winds will be a factor
today – especially if walking
downtown.

When risk is quantified, it shifts
the burden of proof.

The vernacular of insecurity: quick
to correct, slow to establish.

Clues sought across town from the
scene of the crime. Why not?

Sectors with words, sectors with
randomly intersecting lines,
sectors with numbers, sectors in
various colors.

Unanimous, propitious, unaware.

Variations in the loops of the
tangle. And the circumstances.

Every decisive moral vision must
be based on history.

A part of the original design but never built

The Secret History (Procopius)

Doctrines, practices, and structures under a waning star

Dead bodies filling lookout towers or thrown into an enormous ditch newly dug around the walls of Constantinople [543 AD]

Mare Nostrum

Backwards and forwards inconclusively –
making of orderly existence a vehicle of mystery
They said *Yes*
Then they said *Well, yess*
Then they said *Well . . .*
Then they said *No.*

Nailing in the doors and the windows
He reached the cause and effect of the recorded whim – but had no idea whether he had got it right or wrong. Neither the easy acceptance nor the deferred rejection made it any clearer.

Skeptical not only of the soup but also the bowl in which it sat.

Unlocalized

Old gravitas – its high pitches faint and distant

Body, speech, and mind

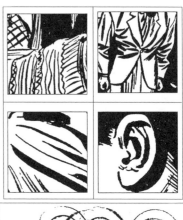

More of a welcome – but no more than a welcome . . .hardly an answer to a question

Standing in the shadows just to see what was lost and what was found

Guess work
Blank at the edges
But diamond hard inside
Something confined like all enigmas
to the riddle of the light

Ragged polygons
flutes and whistles
drums cymbals
and Isaiah-plucked strings

THE JOURNEY ENFORCED –
its creaking and rattling
gathers momentum
at the outset, then settles
into a dispersed rhythmic
clanging as the progress plods
and swells forward

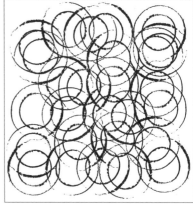

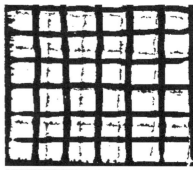

APRIL 9

The effects of water, heat, and cold on oxides of iron and manganese

Reaching the turn –
a full length arrival
all across the skin
all the way to the end

Torque

"an image of informal gravity"
(Pynchon)

Extravagant – and all the more so for having been devised on the spot – half the face in shadow, the other entering a crack in the wall – a guess not made, an answer offered instead

The scorpion and the fox –
Snake wolf bear dog

A single 75 watt bulb
A recurrent oddity

Purcell's Dido, not the Dido of an elegant 'Analysis'

But also free of other forms of human life

Conscience sets its terms in the future perfect where
Ambition accomplishes peripeteia

The objective: travel
The letdown: an anchor pulled behind the first and last wagons leaves a deep line in the sand between the tracks left by the wagon wheels

Overheard on a bus going from 108th Street and Riverside Drive to the Flatiron Building:

"It's warm out. I'm sweating. I'm going to Coney Island next week. They have chairs there for sitting. Next week I'll go. It's warm out there. Sometimes I walk slow all the way to Brighton Beach. It's like money. There's no explaining it. 260 pounds and dead at 72. I know a man on the Upper East side. 79th Street. He stands on his head for 2 hours every day. 97 years old. Everybody calls him 'the mayor'. Stands on his head 2 hours every day. 79 years old. They call him 'the mayor.' My aunt dropped dead at 97. Her heart stopped in front of the television. I thought she had overslept. You never know until your life is over. Look, over there. A taxi got all smashed up. What do you think happened? Someone got shot? Robbed? It doesn't matter. Rents are still $6000 a month. You know, you can stand there and say nothing and it's amazing. But I wear Armani and take the bus. I went into Bergdorf Goodman with my mother 35 years ago. She was alive then. Now it's $50,000 for a dress, $1500 for a sweater, $700 for a hat, if you can find one. I have to be at 14th Street by 11:30. I'm never late for an appointment. Never. 61°. 61°. It's warm out. No snow for the past 5 years. I didn't see any myself. It's taken 3 years to redevelop this corner. Do you remember what was here? It never ends. Donald Trump has killed more people than Hitler. Millions of dollars for a cup of coffee. Homeless people begging in the streets. Not me. I was diagnosed with a borderline personality disorder. Like Marilyn Monroe, like Winston Churchill."

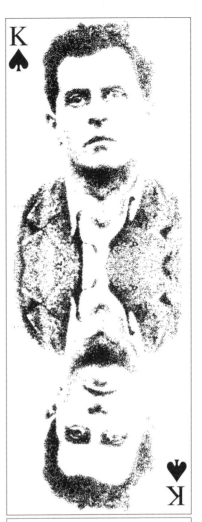

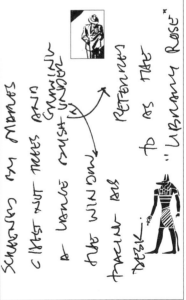

an august daybook

For the looking-glass, originally created for delight — so it was expounded — had become an instrument of anxiety like the clock, which is a compensation for the failure of our activities to follow each other in a natural way.

—Robert Musil, THE MAN WITHOUT QUALITIES

August 1, 2005

I move more slowly now
because there is no one to go with me.
Once again the contrarian has reclaimed
a part of my temperament and demeanor –
back again, back again as always

LAWS AND SMELLS
5000 precedents
100000 footnotes

If you follow the tunnel 200 yards to the east
you'll come to a shaft that leads to an access ladder –
the chamber should be right above you.

9 establishes the depth of the grain 9
from shamanic invocation and germination of the herd
to recorded testament – grown brittle in the withering light

Nowhere to hide because of what
the witness reinvented and added to the story

WHAT THE FAT MAN SAID
From next time to next time
From longshot to long shot
It's all good, it's all physics

Three of the best
then three more
and a final three

Spending a last few scruples for overture –
lost codes provide security

From the fourth to the ninth
9 *is* as 9 *per* – not provident,
beyond clearly tenable reliance –
but offered in evidence

August 2, 2005

Solitary constraints, bewilderment, and other aspects of being . . .

An inconsolable awareness of the finite – especially amid that which has merely been found and not achieved –

What diminished capacity, what lack of human grace compels it?

[Art = The refined implementation of an intuited sense of craft –]

Unavoidably contractile, but sustained, done before the voices stir – everything huddled and flourishing, even the stink. With a dispatching assent – bodies within an inch of shadow, partition in extremis, a tranquil grin behind the murmured hypothesis, so this is the plan of action, this is all that goes before, this is the simplifying regimen and figment probe to ponder –

Handle, hammer, lever, hollow shaft –

Coughing out the wager –

Fuck the posthumous! We want to sit down, eat, and drink sometime today!

Doing business on the street: 4 books turn into 2 books turn into 4 books –

Chromatic and noncommittal as the mountains at sunset –

ECHOING MICHELET: Born during the terror of Fascism, I witness, before I die, the terror of Islam.

A margin of nettles and loosestrife – attendant and impersonal –

Traces of birdsong recede into the distant sound of a train whistle –

Respected though he was it didn't keep many from considering him odd – even, at times, bizarre –

What day is it? Can you tell me what day it is? Not a number – a name. I came back – returning to this particular spot – only to put this here. Do you recognize it?

August 3, 2005

SURVIVAL KIT: Swiss army knife, duct tape, a piece of charcoal, and a wad of paper.

Touching the tip of the wave with your tongue—

Dollar bills folded into the shroud—whims of pious ennui

OPERATIVE WORDS OF THE DAY: Lethal, adaptive, and able to move freely—

A satchel full of taut agendas still waiting to be proofread—

Something dangerous to humans is spreading yet again from Siberia—

The commandment under consideration turned out to be a series of anagrams that ended with a two word question. Its decipherment and application were meant to impel action. The intention was to dismantle the word trophy and thereby expand it.

DESCENDANTS DESTROY VALUE

I will feed you, I will clothe you, I will provide temporary shelter for you—and even give you money. But I will no longer negotiate these letters and lettershapes in the conventional way you suggest. And no you can't take them away and do with them as you please. I don't have a gun, but I do have a knife, or, even better—a bottle of ink to pour over the pages of the whole enterprise. All this was done in the way it was done because it was meant to confound the validity of anything freehand—so your memory will do you no good. Only I know how these things came to be exactly as they now are.

HOBBES BLOT

AUGUST 4, 2005

DEFENSE: SUSPECT
CONTACT: SUSPECT

Arranged by a voice only –

A cycle of respiration interrupted by a seven word spasm –

[PULSE: FIGMENTS INTRUSIFS]

At the morgue, who does all the talking?
Is there anyone else we should be looking at?
Anyone else we should be listening to?

Every deal was worked from a pay phone on Lispenard. But the circuit ran from Spring to Bleecker to Delancey with Bowery running south as the eastern leg. It wasn't until later that it ripened in the opposite direction with Greenwich Street running south as the western leg – but everything was still controlled from the payphone on Lispenard. Drops and anonymous symbol-chalkings could now be made at any point along the route in either direction, especially where it was known that building supers hosed the sidewalks and general areas every morning. In winter it was left to the snow or foot traffic to effect erasure.

ANYTHING WITHIN REACH: Fruitless bathos a priori – [das *un*fruchtbare Bathos a priori] – 'bathos' suggesting a primary sense of 'depth' *not* banal sentiment.

The conscious agent of his own flawed syntheses, he had no confidence in the strength of his chains – much less in what they kept attached to him.

Scripta Manent
Etch CETERA.

AUGUST 5, 2005

The Chinese believe it's bad form to give someone a clock as a gift—reminder that it is of one's mortality. In the past month my former wife has given me 2 clocks that once belonged to her recently deceased mother. [Finocchio, finocchio, / Non dami il mal occhio.] [Schiatta mal occhio / E non più avanti.]

Reread the July 16-31 daybook/e-mail. Awkward & some repetitive phrasing therein at certain points. Small enough to be annoying now that copies are in the hands of both Vincent & PV. Made two minor revisions & reprinted the pages in both sets archived. To repeat: *Schiatta mal occhio / E non più avanti.* Then did these collages

 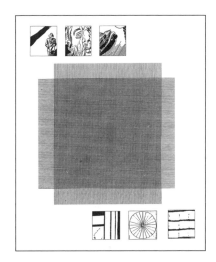

The old man and the boy stood holding hands at the crossroads, their battered shoes sunk almost to the top of the laces into the sand along the side of the road. Earlier they had taken shelter from the sun under a large oak tree thirty yards from where they were now standing. But they had moved out from under the tree almost an hour ago so as not to miss the possibility of someone seeing them and stopping to pick them up as they headed south. The boy could see a shimmering light rise from the lake in the distance where they had spent the night before. He mentioned it to the old man who, as he released the boy's hand from his own, shifted the dusty bag they had between them but said nothing. After a minute or two the boy took the old man's hand again. He looked up the road to the north and hoped a car or truck would soon come by and offer them a ride. The old man began to mutter and repeat softly to himself: "Cristo Cristiello! Tu sei buono, ma è più buono quello. Cristo Cristiello! Tu sei buono, ma è più buono quello." It was something he had heard the old man do before and thought it was a prayer meant to bring someone – anyone – in a vehicle that would take them at least part way to where they wanted to go.

August 6, 2005

Like those patches of red and green and yellow in the painter's art
so too these words and ideas lifted and juxtaposed from
the spoken life set in motion this jagged formation that designates
and is more than enough – despite its lack of logical reconciliation

週刊 生活

Anxious, futile, and irrevocable
the first cut is already made
but not the trim that corrects
the angle and span – stripping
the composed and servile
shadow of its imagined reach

Atlases, encyclopedias,
diaries, annals, maps,
lithographs, letters,
newspapers, and journals

One on the right four on the left
two behind three straight ahead
small shifts minor changes further
conjurings of emphasis – a conscious
agent of his own syntheses – a part of
but never belonging

PALACIO
Both a labyrinth and a lens
A niche of silence and remorse
Lost in translation

Limning an obscure assize
he arrives at an unintended paradox
and determines a mute protagonist
whom he abandons in favor of a blind one
in order to subvert the sources of admission

Having exacted this adaptation from privacies and
tumult and having risen from the murky depths
and proceeded from the cloudy heights and so on
to subsequent maneuvers and contentions of the
narrated remains ever burdened with overstated
lacunae and this Pythagorean throttling

This must be where they mourn for the dead
Unconsoled and grounded in resolve
The spillover steadied only by the proof of breathing
Sentimental songs in envelopes trimmed in black
Pensum-echoed secrets reaching for a name
The peevish monad and subtle adjustment
The captured have been interrogated but
The weeds offer shelter that reaches only to the knees
Millennia pass and you eat an orange
These are the corrections of desire
Millennia pass

August 7, 2005

Talismanic carvings – but to what effect?
A cigarette in a gloved hand . . . fades into the foreground –

Pages blowing across a rain-swept highway. Faces illuminated by a flashing red light, a close-up of a man's hand, then darkness. Everything is in order. A description meant to be caressed.

Going from hand to hand
it ends uncomplicated –
rudimentary amazement
tumbling into a vacuum –
nothing that can be replaced is of value.

The deductions of a movie-goer as he settles into his seat at the matinee
and waits for the credits to roll. He'd just eaten a two dollar lunch at
the counter of the drugstore two doors up: a ham and cheese sandwich,
a slice of apple pie with ice cream, and two cups of coffee –
maybe after the movie it might be good to take a steam and get a shave.

Determination achieves what can now be refused.
"Not just you, and not just you, and not just you, but you, and you, and you, and, especially – you."

Doughnuts and icewater
A December grave
Sulphur torches thrown lit into the Tiber
The drinker's grudge against the size of his glass
Or the space between his fingers
The encounter with *ambages* resistant to transcendence
The inwardness of the maze becomes intuition
Tangled orbits inhabit all that is reconciled
Through repeated doors and similar chambers
From narrow path to smooth road to narrow path
All cards on the table all fingers on the triggers
Prayer tablets attached to the branches of trees moving in the wind.
Meaningful acquisitions corrected to read *meaningful insights*.
– Hanging from a blue nail –

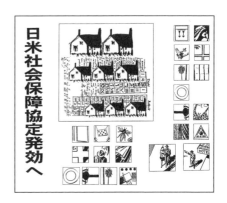

STILL AVAILABLE FOR USE
Dionysian
Orphic
Mithraic

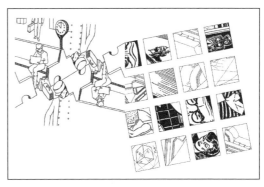

– The preestablished *because* as an adjunct to seriality:
The argument unicursal or multicursal –
Where then?
Beyond or below – but neither absolute.

We're over the western horizon now and there's no sign of Odysseus or Prospero. The facts and the way they are arranged are only of nominal interest. No distinction is made between history and myth though both as always play a part in the nature of each. 'Wehweh,' sagt Wittgenstein. 'Weh nach Weh,' sage ich. 'Von Weh zu Weh – in einem Zug.' Independent of the mechanism. *Das Innere* – beyond the numen of lexical afflatus. A beckoning side street –

Sunday was another one of those days when I didn't venture out at all. I think I'm in need of rescue of some sort. The book that interests me most these days is THE IDEA OF THE LABYRINTH by Penelope Reed Doob. I've always been in love with the fragmented prospect of the maze-walker. I obsessively drew them freehand as a kid – and now I write them and make collages that allude to their replication. In 1990 I wrote something called INDISCRETIONS OF THE MINOTAUR. It was one of the first pieces I wrote on the computer and not a typewriter. There he was – where you'd expect to find him – sequestered in the handiwork of Daedalus. Any reference to Ariadne and her thread wasn't even a consideration in the pages I wrote. Though Daedalus had left his name on the walls – the letters of which were taken through various permutations--as tho he'd signed his work in a series of 'Killroy Was Here' assertions all to be found recorded in one place only – just in case the minotaur should at some point wander through this particular passageway. Variants of the artist's signature as antagonistic as a piece of graffiti. [The French word for 'labyrinth' is 'dédale'].

Roll in, roll wide, roll deep, roll often.

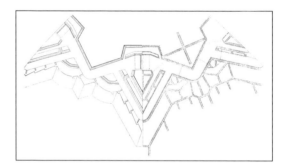

I woke up this morning with you on my mind.
It's funny how sweet dreams can be so unkind.

Queste Pagine
Questi Scritti
Questo Saltarello

Everything on edge
Nothing at the edges

I'm looking for an italic font that leans to the left.

An extended murmur – spiking occasionally on a recognizable syllable – offered in evidence –

"Say a prayer for me. Tuesday was always my lucky day. I'm telling you this on Thursday. So now you have plenty of time to do what I ask."

Another crack-up on Circus Street –

Flattening in the direction of acceleration –

Unaccountable echoes in the bare rafters –

I think the Jack of Diamonds is missing.

Given rapid and persistent cellular change are you yourself? Now? Now? How about now? And *now?*

When you feel your weight do your eyes glow. How about her – when she feels your weight? What about *her* eyes.

It was his mind. It was that. It was his mind. It wasn't that it wasn't proper made up about the matter – it was that his *mind* wasn't properly *made*. If it had once been, it no longer was.

Part of the de-orbit burn involved looking for a pen, and when one was finally located replacing it with one that had sufficient ink in the cartridge. The critical part was scheduled to happen at 10:04 am Eastern Time. Crowds began gathering in Secaucus.

No matter how hard the scribe worked, no matter how sharp, or how wide, or how tall, or how elegant his letters were, the speaker continued to pronounce elite 'ill-lit'.

It's only theory, only speculation, that you were used simply for dissemination. They figured that when you were done *communicating*, maybe *then* you'd have something to say.

"I don't care if you were told one thing and then shortly thereafter told something quite to the contrary. It's up to you, and it will always be up to you, that after assessing all the raw data, all the information – whatever you choose to call it – that you personally *always* make the right choices – even if you lie and it means you have to tell them that these choices were made purely on the basis of intuition alone."

At the beginning the day itself dominated – but soon what was said about the day took precedence.

Another primordial landscape, one in which only the occasional Joshua tree was to be seen in any direction.

He poured a drink, sat on the bed, and handed her a lit cigarette
Her blue eyes darkened noticeably as she exhaled smoke from a corner of her mouth –

Not only received information and logistical support but placement
of the camera was now part of the military action
– and there was a book, or something about *'a book on the subject',*
I believe was the operative phrase at the time of our conversation –

Anybody or somebody, anywhere or somewhere, anytime or sometime
within the capacity of this dimension – he was of three minds, at least,
in the shaping: imperfect, clamoring, and scattered – scattering imperfectly
the clamor – the rose trapped within the crocus confines the bee's *on dit* –
formal, sad, genial, and full of octaves – these are the attributes we set against
all others, neither more or less essential because they are immediate – their
inner distinctions consist of moral experience or deftly intuited contrivance

It is generally agreed . . . it is also agreed . . . nevertheless it is hoped –
Confrontational language and the struggles for power on secondary levels –

I found the Jack of Diamonds, maybe it was there all along; but now it's the Queen of Hearts that's missing.

WORN, TORN, SPLIT,
SPLINTERED, BROKEN,
LOOSE, SHAKEY, SAGGING,
WEAK, MISSING,
SCRATCHED, STAINED,
WARPED, JAMMED, STUCK.

Thinking posthumously – at least at the moment. The cartouche inscribed with evidence of its own corrosive nature. An animated and integral blemish. It acquits the virtuously adversarial like a dirge. *From Black to* Black – Kali, merci.

The mordant invocation of the undetermined world is recognized, albeit only partially, in the successful ironies that brighten its contours and darken its interior, drawing for emphasis on the corrupted allusions and insinuations of manifest and debilitated attention.

It just wouldn't burn – I needed more time.

You can talk to it and talk to it all you want – and nothing will probably happen. But if you dance with it for a while, something may develop. And I don't just mean that if you caper long enough your ass will fall off.

The music holds back for a while, repeating already developed minor phrases before the inevitable expression of the larger thematic strains.

A counterpoint not of imposition but of adaptation –

The so-called permanent emotions: heroic, erotic, wondrous, mirthful, sorrowful –

Dead ends that taunt –

Things that are hard to see are hard to count –
at least in any conventional way

The hoaryzontal

I went and they were all gone – an old wide awake
hat and an old straw bonnet of the plumb pudding s
ort were left behind – I put the hat in my pocket
thinking it might be usefull for another oppertunity –
as good luck would have it, it turned out to be true

Not now, not ever, not at all . . .

Along a ledge that stretched to the entrance of a small cave in the icewall –

He buttonholed me along the upper reaches of Broadway near Columbia. I hadn't seen him in more than 10 years. He recognized me first and stepped in front of me as I headed downtown. "You shaved your beard," he said. "That don't make a damn bit of difference. I go to church and say my prayers regularly. Wait until you see what I can do when I'm 75. I'll be able to do more than you can now. And you're only 60. Right?" I told him it was good to see him, gave him five bucks, and continued on my way. He waited until I'd walked about 10 paces and then shouted, "You always were a prick!" It didn't look like he had much time left.

AUGUST 11, 2005

She brought out what she called the 'misery spoons' and
put them next to our plates. "We each get one," she said.
An old monk had told me that the last time he ate with her
she had wrapped his fork in a 20 dollar bill before he sat down.

What are the reaches of the page –
Their original purpose now forgotten after so much revision
Intent upon such accuracy of address –
First testing the new pen on a scrap of paper
Before making an initial entry in the new notebook –
The imagined face around the eyes
As though something were diminished by being
Brought into sharper focus – the four dimensional object
That casts a three dimensional shadow

I failed to sleep soundly and had a very uneasy dream. I thought my wife lay on my right arm and somebody took her
away from my side which made me wake up very unhappy. I thought as I awoke somebody said 'Bess' but nobody was
near. I stretched out again with my head towards the north to show myself the steering point in the morning –

It's not the evidence but the 'rules of evidence' that skew the decision toward death –
Unlike the recorded particulars – explored but left unexplained – the rest is real

The Interpreter's Song

Inside the inside is a contraption that runs the gimmick –
The road very often looked as strange as myself and I was barely half-awake as I went –
Everything was tasted only that the water that followed prove more refreshing –

A disciplined compassion rather than a compassionate discipline –
Marked by a polite lack of understanding on each side
In an effort to avoid, or perhaps merely forestall, a direct statement of opinion.

– with the addition to the post-mortem of a broad smile and an unspoken accusation – but, taken together, it all
seemed nothing out of the ordinary. The relation between things had shifted only slightly. Almost any other set
of details would have brought about the same effect. Granted there existed an acceptance of the possibility – or
rather, the *opportunity*, to make mistakes on a daily basis – no other sense of resolve to the contrary.

Certain things were put out of sight each time he went out, slippers, bathrobe, pajamas, bandages, tape, various
books – envelopes were placed with their addresses face down, and the bedroom door was shut against the
often unmade bed, the rolled-up oriental rug, and the room's general disorder. Wastebaskets were emptied
and no dishes remained in the sink. All this was accomplished most afternoons by around 1 in case he should
encounter someone interested enough to return with him to the apartment.

August 12, 2005

At some point I will make this
clearer to you *outloud* –

Once it was furtive glances,
bad shoes, and the smell of
garlic on the breath – now it's
abandoned packages and
generally suspicious behavior
in public places where
movement is confined –

What about those eight nuns
sitting at the sushi bar?

Sovereignty in remote places
continues to depend on use –

A lengthy consideration of the visible sign leads you to think – what? Major issues remain? Names? Places? Things overheard or only partially understood? Time to kill the messenger and the scribe who prepared what was delivered, equalling or even surpassing any rhetorical adjustment. Time to go back to the beginning.

A classic? Sure it's a classic – but only in retrospect. In the past it was just part of the background with a publicity still to mark the date.

Above the roar of the machines what do the words "The best they can do" really mean? Something on the reverse? Something deemed profitable for all concerned? These are the points at which the entrepreneurial crosses the auspicious and sinister – the places where notoriety and emotionless greed had been most successful. And now? What was the giveaway? Who tripped over the dropped shoe?

A hydra of independent convictions meant to conceal profoundly spiritual shortcomings – and what had seemed ideal exertions in the cause of personal diplomacy – the rush of engagement was always addictive

Briefings and rehearsals ran through all echelons of command and led to demoralizing results –

Always moving around the edges of the variants, never distracted, never venturing closer than necessary – a ceremony without resolution, full of its own *eccentricities* –

On the west side of midnight –
The Queen of Hearts and now
The Ace of Diamonds – I know
Coyote's got them and I'm sure
He's got some ideas of his own

With margins adjusted and the 3 placed only as close to the 1 as necessary –
[noting in this how the lens continues to work at least in one particular way]

I Vespri Siciliani, La Forza Del Destino – such natural choices as background
while tracing the options of origin – still dressed in rags – only Hearts and Diamonds –
around such minima the focus is sharpened within a spatial balance unique to every page

As Elihu said unto Berzelius, and Alexander unto many, putting laughter into the code,
[in the spirit of Christopher Smart *For he is tenacious of his point*] –
Bold from his instruction by Hermes and further named by Autolycus:
'this our paunch before still bears them, faithful, no mere dog's whim,
for I have dined where all the learned shall at the labor stand
and Raymond like a Sallee rover lent his soft obstetric hand –'

Silence or nervous laughter attends,
Pucked in profile – no syllable disrupted –
For every family had one cat at least in the bag.

– Inscriptions Over the Gate to a Potters Field

The past commits the future in making a present of the past –
Das Gift, indeed, despite any subversion of the routes taken in its acquisition –
because anything *bestowed* should be noted with suspicion
– for protection mark it in red as well as any instruction to do so –
[The arrow is straight, but its aim confounded]

Inscriptions Over the Gate to a Potters Field
– but who else would come here with such evidence?
The cause behind the effect is not the right approach –
I run, they chase, they run, I chase, consistent with the rest of the conjugation.
Caught on some unidentifiable scruple I would be hard pressed to say which I prefer

I know these things because muted renditions were performed prior to the record being made – though I
can't say exactly when. *[I got up early and started writing immediately & then lost track of time – tho not the fact
that G. was to be with me today – I'll need 20 minutes to get ready – can I meet you at the Garden of Eden at 10:30?]*
Anticipation, inevitability, and lust – compounded by the etiquette of mutual avoidance. [*I Stretti* – pushed ever
closer and closer to relieve emphasis.]

He sat on his hat and took another pluck from the bottle in the bag. He told me he had been a clown in the
circus and had gone by the professional name *A Fortiori*. Now he was traveling eastwards, and always carried a
deck of cards.

August 14, 2005

Though I turn no one away,
with my increasing privacies
I become more of a stranger –
but my personal landscape becomes
more complex and elaborately expressed –
isolating place, connection, and the dream
of a social reality is now directed by another
set of determinants – the words are
not written but pressed into the paper,
the process slowed in order to refine
and better shape the ideas being realized –
anywhere begins everywhere
everywhere begins anywhere – neither
realization is a benign one – what they
observe is loss and its subsequent contrivances –
place begins where there is insufficient detail,
it ends and is finally abandoned for the same reason –
what remains is usually only a report of survivors,
noting the same leafless tree so oddly located
behind the filling station or the snowdrifts that
cover the bodies or piles of frozen shoes –
have you been here before, will you come here again?

She dropped to her knees, leaned forward, and lifted her skirt over her ass all in one movement. No panties. Supporting herself with her left hand she reached with the right for the cigarettes on the coffee table next to her. He slipped his dick into her ass and slowly started fucking her. She smoked and he fucked. When he finished and stepped away from her she told him she was out of cigarettes and was thinking about switching brands. He pulled up his pants and left the room. She didn't bother turning around to see what he looked like.

BRIDGING OPTIONS & IMPLEMENTING STRATEGIES [THOUGH I'M ALWAYS HAPPY NOT TO BE NEEDED]
"If I make a move and you flinch your ass is mine. If I make a move and you flinch your ass is *anyone's.*"
This judgement behooves the longer and harder – no matter the timeline. The principles remain the same.

$215 BILLION & 5000 LIVES LOST
Squandered opportunities and lowered expectations –
consistency exists only where mistakes are being made.
Faceless, the illusory autonomous are waiting for a piece of the action.
This, to those running the show, is appropriate and only to be expected.

The traces that remain can only be characterized as runic
And, though obviously mannered, their basic intent was cautionary –

Points of intersection like big ugly scars – place leads to place –
progress evolves and the momentum fragments. The air is not fresh
at the turning points. Blowing sands . . . Ambiguous messages and
confusing pressures – for now let's call it a minor development –
the item in question has been detained in transit –

AUGUST 15, 2005

38 YEARS
Waiting in the sun, he watched as the trucks pulled away. "No more gazebo in Gaza," Rajah remarked. "No more gazebo in Gaza – no more nothing," added his son.

RAW FOOTAGE
"I'll believe that when the pig fucks the cat."

CREATURE COMFORTS
An interesting line of work, no one on top,
big chair, thick rugs, no traps,
no one else on top.

INCIDENTS OF TRAVEL
"Go home now. I'll call you later. Take care of the dog. Make sure there's water in his bowl. Feed him. You'll find an envelope with some money in the knife drawer. Just do like I say. Feed the dog first because he can't open the can."

"Tell me something. All that bad news you've been getting, does it come to you only when you're asleep? Or when you're hanging upside down? You should try writing some of it down and showing it to a few people who know about these things. I'm sure there's more than a few of them out there. Maybe one of them can help you sort it out. In the meantime, you shouldn't spend so much time inside. It's better to sweat. That air conditioning will only fuck up your head even more."

MARK IT
From the meander to the grid, all patterns enthuse – suggesting another measure might be cut from previous discernments. Renewal – fragment upon fragment, the lone trace clarified beyond any already developed complex. This now is a complexion of its own – every hum, hiss, and bark as solvent as never heard before.

BEARDS IN THE LIMO
"You have here a constituency of opportunists. Spoilers – fashioning a template for anarchy and terror. Apart from money and weapons nothing else is deliverable – at least for now."

THE ILLUSORY AND AUTONOMOUS ARE WAITING FOR A PIECE OF THE ACTION
The traces that remain can only be characterized as *runic*. And though obviously somewhat mannered in design, it's evident their basic intent was cautionary, addressed as they were from the extremes.

A MIX OF THE CONGENIAL AND PROFANE
Just as might be said, just as might be felt – a place to take whatever else you have.

THE LAST GRAND OPENING
"How about it there, Tertullian? Let's open all the windows and breathe some outside air. What do you say? Let the louvers rattle, my friend, let the louvers rattle."

INCIDENTS OF TRAVEL II

"You don't take a bath, or shave, or brush your teeth for two weeks. You sleep in the same clothes every day. You keep a bottle of vodka in the refrigerator and have a $3000 bike hanging from the ceiling. All you talk about is the cia and the Arabs. From that you want me to think you know something about the street? You're just a bullshit asshole, a 58 year old schoolboy. Never mind – take a bath, brush your teeth, change your clothes, wipe your ass – you fucking stink."

"Tell me, Jessop – and we're just testing the waters here – who is this lardass sodomite whose patter has you so enthralled? What are you going to tell me next – that this brown-eye mule-loper is running a bigger show than anyone else? You don't know what the fuck you're talking about. You don't even know who the fuck you are."

THE MEASUREMENT FRANCHISE
More than the sum of its parts – especially
when influence exceeds ownership.

ROUGH NOTES [PUNCTUATED] NON SE QUIT UR – *OR*, YOUR SHOES MAKE A STICKY SOUND WHEN YOU WALK
　　Take your time with this water. It's very cold. Take your time. Bring the glass to your mouth slowly. And as you
　　drink let the water cover the entire top of your tongue before it hits the back of your throat. Take your time.

A mix of the congenial and the profane – just as might be said, just as might be felt – a place to to take whatever you had left. ☐ Who should I be? And when? And where? Who should I be? And why? I won't be fooled again. Why? Because I won't be fooled again. ☐ Lowlifes climbing in and out of the Golden Triangle – all smart enough to find their way around the money. ☐ It now seems I have only the slightest reason to move in the next or any direction. These and other words keep me more or less rooted to the spot. I must be waiting for someone who doesn't know I'm here. ☐ What I expected to find was something like a room in an old-fashioned men's club – with large leather chairs, oriental rugs, heavy draperies, and small mahogany tables with a glass and a bottle of brandy in easy reach on every one. Instead I found a room with rough, unpainted floors, a single arrowback chair, and an upright piano – the only light coming from a single 40 watt bulb hanging from the ceiling ☐ Caligari-inspired unities employed to make sense of it all – gaps occurring spontaneously between the handwritten lettershapes. The words balanced like a sharpshooter leaning forward into a stiff wind. No way to differentiate left from right, so both are suggested. ☐ Only anecdotal details remain, many of them improvised on the spot, before the houselights go up and the curtain rises. ☐ My interrogator was one who found himself to be fair-minded despite the obvious lack of respect he had for the man he was questioning. He had an instinct for both when it came to 'a person of interest'. Was this someone who came late or someone who lingered after the others had gone in order to do his damage without distraction or witnesses. ☐ Neutral postures further submerged in chastened sensuality – ☐

TUMBLING DICE — A GEOMETRY
Part One: The Hazard
   No return to the white space from the white space

Words, parts of words, fragmentary phrases, lengthy and complex sentences – some of which were carefully punctuated – elaborate mathematical computations indicative of the application of careful procedures evolving into ever more detailed numeric and symbolic discernments – written everywhere, covering every surface in the hallway and all three rooms, covering the walls, the floors, doors, the drapes, blank pages in books, paintings, the bedding, shirts, trousers, the surfaces of appliances--every available space in the entire apartment elaborately marked with testamentary devotion.

Part Two: Rigors of the Zone
   A return from the black space to the white

Not an empire but a commercial republic – first distinction of the morning. ["The word labyrinth comes from 'labor' and intus'. -Nicholas Trevet] To distinguish competence: a labyrinth that has an exit but no entrance. Is it music or the accomplished pull of the bow across the strings? Four sides + a top and a bottom – all bearing specific numerical indicators. A minimum of two objects of this description are required. The first phase of the architecture being planned occurs while both are in midair. [A cyclic complexity augmented by the divergent and episodic.] The hand that held them now awaits a further purpose.

Part Three: Domus Dedaly
   Turning from the white space to the black

Though relevant, lythe [easy] and swevenes [dreams] clear the system of any lexical importunings. Such distinctions establish placement, albeit ambiguous, somewhere within the complex of cursi. There a pillar, here a ramp, there a smooth bend, here a sharp angle, a flight of stairs, handholes, cobbled areas, areas paved smooth, a basket raised or lowered to various levels by rope, doorways, halkes and hurnes, overhangs, ledges, beams, pilings, chambers, gates, moated termini –

Part Four: Imposture and Stealth
   No turnings

At rest one side is always invisible – unless viewed from beneath through a transparent surface. A more universal pov is required to sustain the momentum. Inertia inhabits every reflective pause.

Part Five: Immersion in Tacit Contradictions
   Torsion as mass

What is to be measured by and accounted purpose in the numeric statement arrived at? Does this affirm inertia?

Part Six: Beyond Axiom or Analogue
   A return to the white space via black

[What is now face down?]

August 18, 2005

PEOPLE I'VE FORGOTTEN

Alan Austin, Rae Koppert, Gary & Judee Brone, Michael Collard, Joey Calnan, Paul Coopersmith & Prue Page, Christine Demetriadi, Stefan Daagarson, Ray Freed, Jane Grove, Barbara Greenberg, Karen Bunjer-Gulden, Claude Gill, Mitzi Jones, S.H. Kaplan, Eva Kamasa, John Marron, David Mayor, N. Littlewood, John Robinson, Gilbert Reid, Lasse Söderberg, John Barton Epstein, Tony Ward, John Wierwille, J. Harris, Mike Burford, Margaret Okuma, Bill Wertheim, Hans Oldewarris, Linda Whitmore, and Gabriella Bianchini.

THREE ON THE CORNER

A middle-aged black guy in a wheelchair was in heated conversation with his friend who was selling used books and salvaged household items from a table on Broadway & 109th Street. Every third sentence he spoke was "All we have to do is figure out how to manufacture the motherfuckers." I had no idea what he was in reference to and probably neither did his friend who went on pretending to listen intently and at the same time trying to interest me in some of his wares. I bought a book from him; and while money changed hands his friend in the wheelchair continued his harangue, cool in the shade of a junk tree, staring straight ahead and repeating the phrase of the day: "All we have to do is figure out how to manufacture the motherfuckers."

ALIGHTING

Distraction dressed in white
distraction dressed in red
distraction dressed in blue
distraction dressed in green
distraction dressed in luminous distraction

EARNESTLY REASONED

Shouts in the street – misplaced
contempt – we are actually in retreat –
blown back one explosion at a time – only
two perspectives remain – even established
motives are suspect – finality merely
a doled predictive pattern of closure –
something mechanical left behind to signal
what else might remain – approaching
through grasses and plumes of smoke

THE RED PYRAMID AND MANO CORNUTO

The real constitution of things is accustomed to hide itself.
—Heraclitus

You could wear this pyramid like a badge – but it must be red and hidden under your shirt, or pinned to the lining of your jacket, or placed in one of your pockets.

With the index and little fingers extended and the middle two fingers folded and held down by the thumb you can then waggle the 2 protruding fingers like a set of horns. Or you can use them to poke out the eyes of the jettatore – or whomever you think is giving you the mal occhio.

– People seldom say what they mean. But I do. And I think you can tell that I do by the tone of my voice. I'd like to know what you're thinking – in order to add it to my point of view. Not so much to expand my outlook, but to allow what you disclose to be there as a possible point of reference – an adjunct, let us say, to some moment of required mediation in which these thoughts you might now share with me could function in an altogether different way. Of course the choice is yours – nevertheless it is one that might lead to the opportunity to be part of the future in a way never anticipated by either of us.

There is much here that is profane – but it is something whose inflections and verbalizations I have chosen to explore – at least for the present. Many will have heard worse and many will have heard nothing at all – which might, in the latter instance, better sustain their own private purpose and consequence.

No populist rhetorician – was there ever one? – he had long ago turned from emotion to grammar –

Fama malum quo non aliud velocius ullum – No other evil travels faster than gossip [and the further it goes the stronger it becomes]
—Publius Vergilius Maro

FOR THE DEFENSE

How dumb is this motherfucker? You're asking *me* how dumb this motherfucker *is*? I'll tell you how damn dumb this motherfucker is. This motherfucker don't know Idaho from Egypt. That's how goddamn dumb this motherfucker is. So don't ask me again.

THEME WITH VARIATION

How dumb is this motherfucker? Is that what you're asking me? How goddamn motherfuck dumb he *is*? Is that what you want to know? That's what *you* want *me* to explain to you? Well I'll tell you how fucking dumb this motherfucker is. He don't know motherfucking Idaho from motherfuck Egypt—that's how fucking dumb he is. So don't ask me again.

THEME WITH VARIATION II

How goddamn dumb is this poor motherfucker? Is that what you want me to motherfuck *tell* you? To start with, how motherfucking dumb are *you*? This motherfucker don't know shit stain Idaho from piss stain Egypt. That's how damn dumb this poor motherfucker is. That's how *fucking dumb*. So don't *ask* me again. You know what I mean, you *other* dumb motherfucker?

DRESSING PROPERLY FOR THE RIGHT OCCASION

The cop shot him through the head. Right through the fucking head. The poor bastard was just standing there and the cop walked up, pulled out his gun. and shot him through the fucking head. I mean he had his hat on—and it still went through his head and out the fucking other side. Hat or no hat. And the cop was a brother too. Maybe that's why he did it. Pulled out his big ass cop gun. Boom. One shot. Just like that. Right through his head. Right through his hat and out the other fucking side of his head. Right fucking through. Boom. *One shot*. You could see it. Two holes in the head, two holes in the hat. He really loved that hat and he told me if anything bad ever happened to him I could have it. Now what fucking good is it? I can't wear it. They ought to make that fucking cop put it on when they lock the sonofabitch up. Pull both his fucking ears through the holes. I wanted that hat.

STATE DEPARTMENT MEMO: EXIT STRATEGY

Talk backwards while walking backwards.

MOUSTAPHA FINNBAR MAHOOD

He said they should all get to their feet. They should stand up like they meant to hold their ground and start singing. That would release their rancor and focus their energies, making them better ready to fight for their lives when the time came. Jazaria played a twelve bar introduction on the piano and everyone stood up.

WHEN SHE WALKED OFF THE STAGE IT WAS LIKE A CAST OF THOUSANDS HAD DEPARTED

"Señor . . . señor, I am sorry, but you see, donkey tired—yes, donkey *very tired*—he work so hard all the time to make you and *everyone* who come here happy."

There were two quite disparate places marked on the map because he was lost. In any case that was what the person who later found the map assumed.

A hand-dug hole five feet across and approximately seven feet deep with steep sides where the earth had been packed hard by the diggers as they shaped the crater, making it difficult to reach the few inches of water at the bottom.

These words are spoken by a king who, while walking in a grove with his beloved wife, loses her by some darkly miraculous occurrence. He then wanders from place to place asking birds and beasts whether they can give him any intelligence about her. On one occasion his questions are addressed to a blind elephant who is being guided by a white tiger.

I saw a tiger coming down from that mountain when I was a very young boy. I asked him what fault had been committed by the deer he had just killed and eaten. He offered no answer. From this I learned a lesson in modesty.

Kings reside in palaces. Rich men live in mansions. Clouds move across the sky. Lotuses grow in water. There are many jewels in the ocean. Monkeys have long tails. There is no medicine for a fool. Parrots fly at the window. A peacock struts beside the palace wall where a beggar asks for money. Mountains shake and stars shine. A red light fills the sky. The city is surrounded by rivers. At the far end of the courtyard in the shade of a large tree a naked girl feeds a deer handfuls of corn. I drank wine instead of water. My books and papers were taken away. Only two stars shone in the east. We did our planting and sowing in the moonlight. Two travelers emerged from the forest adjoining my fields. They spoke a language I didn't understand and offered me two mangoes in payment, I thought, for the right to cross my land. I knew such things were done in foreign places for fear of obstacles.

Honey on the tongue often means poison in the heart. The only lessons that matter are lessons in humility. I taste neither honey nor poison. I am without shame. To some courage might only be an ornament – but valor brings fame. Doubt can be tended like a garden – and fear in the same way. Silence is the best response to arrogance. Little or nothing will come from a challenge that merely seeks a further response. It's better to beg than earn your wealth by another man's labor. One who composes precepts would anoint your eyelids with his tongue.

Most statements are quickly contradicted. This is the cause of their effect. Most statements are quickly contradicted. This is the effect of their cause. Which is the better order in which these statements should be read? How might their assertions best be repudiated?

What you have before you is not a body of evidence but a series of clues. Although your instinctive response would be "of course" – it still remains that important determinations are lacking. All declensions by their very nature are irregular. Similar consonants followed by ever changing vowels and occasional reversals of consonants or unexpected shifts and appearances of altogether new consonants – now become a pattern determined only by default – dentals combined with linguals, palatal with dental and lingual with nasal and palatal – labial with dental and palatal – and lingual with palatal with the aspirate applied to the guttural or labial – vowels added and consonants dropped – consonants replacing vowels and vowels where consonants were expected – subtle inflections are now the only determinants – lexical roots that govern accusatives – verbs implying motion govern the accusative but also in some instances the dative when establishing the place where the motion is directed – further complications arise with verbs implying anger, malice, rivalry, envy and jealousy – depending upon the person or thing against whom or which the feeling is directed –

Many people had arrived. They had come with only one shared purpose – to read the ransom note. An enormous plume of vapor and spray rose from the base of the falls.

Rudeness, impudence, anger, enmity, pain, difficulty, foulness, depravity, addiction, loneliness, sickness, failure, abuse, disease, hostility, impurity, loss, dismay, affliction, despair, censure, abandonment, vexation, contempt, distrust, accusation, dishonor, doubt, torture, betrayal, lies, theft, tedium, fear, rebuke, death, blindness, malice, hunger, repudiation, misery, obstruction, poverty, deceit, curses, meanness, futility contradiction, taunts, corruption, shame, contrivance, restraint, thirst, pollution, fracture, disaffection, chaos, isolation, and greed –

A sentinel structure built of brick, cast iron, brass, marble, slate, bronze, and glass contained a room with a cracked window, torn curtains, unmade bed and stale sheets, clothing strewn in dusty corners or hanging limp from the edges of doors, bags of books, others in precarious stacks, a broken clock, disconnected phone, mute radio, abandoned and mismatched shoes, bureaus with half-open drawers and overflowing contents, framed paintings and faded drawings hanging on the unpainted walls at crazy angles, some behind broken glass, jagged pieces of which remaining where they had long ago fallen to the floor –

Banished from Rome by Domitian in the middle of the second century A.D. he lived in Necropolis where he taught literature and philosophy. Though he left no written book, his ideas were known through the efforts of two of his more famous pupils, The Arizona Kid and the Lone Vaquero of Vienna, who had faithfully recorded his discourses, four of which were later collected in a work titled Encheiridion which summarizes his ideas. The philosophy that was advocated was essentially one of acceptance and endurance.

A rutted patch, once feudal and now a place to end – contorted and face down like an ancestor.

Still in the vocabulary
Still in the shrine –
Or now only in the niche
In the back of the mausoleum –

"Hey, Presto, where's the elephant? And what have you done with the other half of the girl?"

He may have been half-asleep but he was always punctual – his shout could be heard throughout the building – though almost a daily occurrence, it never failed to bring all the inhabitants to a halt. They stood motionless for a moment – for some it always took a second or two to remember what they were about to do or where they were headed – but then they all moved forward again through the slowly fading though undiminished echoes of the shout –

THE EMPHATIC – *Ungoverned*
THE EMPHATIC – *Generative*
THE EMPHATIC – *Contradictory*
THE EMPHATIC – *Protective*
THE EMPHATIC – *Absolving*

AUGUST 23, 2005

A weak conscience bolstered only by a timetable alibi –
Eumolpus reappears with this in addition and that in subtraction

– Despite the volatile but ponderous candor of Behemoth

Celeus welcomed Demeter and Icarius welcomed Dionysus at Eleusis
This is a clear distinction

The same proportions and key angles emerge
From the determining spiral tattooed on the neck of Ogmios
– *thin gold chains linking their ears to the tip of his tongue* –

Said the man once hanging from the branch:

They gave me no bread,
They gave me no mead,
I looked down;
With a loud cry
I took up runes
From that tree I fell.

HOPE AGAINST HOPE ♠ HOPE ABANDONED ♠ NO REASON TO LIVE
These are upright – they are not *the* upright.
Perhaps that's why they remain.

– Where this is first recorded
Where this is first read
Where this is last heard
Are not of consequence
Though this is only as far as the words take us
Based as always on how little is known
And is, in turn, confounded by supposition
– From agon to palimpsest to fragment

The name of the settlement was Errant Lonesome. Population 225. Its most prominent citizen was named George. It was his custom to invent new names for both people and things – especially those people who found themselves only passing through on their way to someplace else. George never asked where they came from, how long they were staying, or where they intended to go when they left. But whenever he saw them, he spoke to them only by the names he had given them.

Unconfirmed rumors said that he first took shelter in a convent, but only long enough for his wounds to be barely attended to. He then went into hiding in a monastery somewhere in the mountains in southern Italy where the abbot had once been a classmate of his when they were young. An old man named Gaetano DeFelice who for many years had helped the nuns with the convent's annual harvest had guided him there. Compounded by this three day's journey south, his injuries were slow to heal. But led by Frater Antonio, the cloister's resident apothecary, the monks took the initiative in tending to the stab wounds, rather than bringing in a physician from one of the small neighboring towns in the valley. It was decided during his stay at the monastery that he would ultimately head further south through Calabria guided by one of the younger monks while traveling only at night and sleeping in caves or seeking shelter at other monasteries along the way. From Calabria he would cross to Sicily with the monk who had accompanied him. From there they would sail together to North Africa where they would join his brother Nicolai who had already been there for more than a year.

Set alone in an open field, as such places invariably are, its inner and outer walls are of paper and canvas and tremble in the slightest breeze – it still suggests a structure that is more than a tent but far less than a shrine. The air is dry, it hasn't rained in months. It seems I've been going in and out of its two doorways for weeks, reading what has been attached along the walls, seeing much that has been written there fading in the sunlight, its edges torn. But I am not the only one who comes here again and again – far from it. I see many of the same faces each day. It's as though by reading what has been placed here one might eventually realize – based solely on these printed and handwritten records – that there is still something more to add. Many pages remain yet to be read. But there are some I return to each day – and on some occasions I will read and reread only those I have read countless times before – sometimes searching for familiar pages before they have faded completely or been carried off by the winds at night.

Narrowed now to these austere dimensions –
with neither grace nor gentleness to enhance its form –
An astonishment – a dwelling place for dragons –

The markings seemed at first
to emerge beyond the referential field
of any cognitive function – possessing
not the logic of stone against stone
nor the logic of stone upon stone
– but a logic of stone within stone

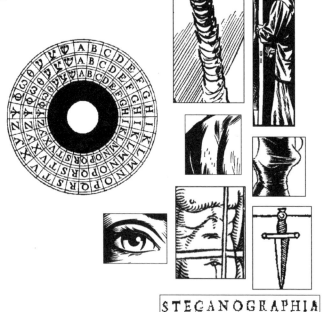

STEGANOGRAPHIA

The pretext for these convictions
is reparation – no other way remains
in which to respond to loss –

The one who was slapped took
a small step forward – not to menace
or to respond in kind, but still surprised
and expressionless, to ask why –

The superstition that covets and would possess
far more than it would keep at bay – this too is
within the nature of a reparation – to take away
what maintains its hold and with which there
is no bargaining – to take away all possibility
of self-protective indirection – and by such desire
forestall even necessary deception –

There is a preponderant complexity to anything that attaches –
What is it you would have me deny?

AUGUST 25, 2005

Neither penitential nor resigned nor ambiguous in her flattery –
She remained tenacious but fragile . . .

No prophetic role – there was always too much retrospect
In the claims for that – too much maneuvering in the present
While burdened with the past – a constant shifting of tenses –
One must *begin* somewhere – where had this *begun* – there
Would be another beginning as there *had been* one in the past.
Were the same people to be there? Who remains? Who was
Missing then? Who is missing now? What of the future?
Questions framed in three languages before determining the one
In which they would best be expressed. A decision that was
Not easily arrived at. A certain dignity had to be maintained.
After all, this was not meant to be some *Maceronicon* –
Should someone take the time to effect a place for it, however
Small and no matter how long it might remain overlooked. Now
Only the words mattered. The issue was straightforward enough.

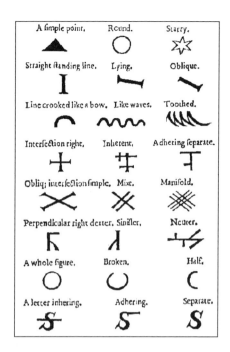

Dear –
  You would further validate all that I write to you by turning as much of it as you
choose to your own purposes – and in any way you prefer. But if I know you as I think I do,
you already see some danger in my merely suggesting this. You know as well as I that certain
absurdities are never to be reconciled but merely observed. Don't burn my letters. Make a start
from them and go on from there as I know only you can. I continue to write to you in this way
remembering what you once said about the affirmation that will always remain beyond disclosure.
You are my Goethe – that's why I send you my imaginary child.
                    With warm regard,
                    M –

["Folly, Melancholy, Madnesse, are but one disease . . . And who is not a Foole, who is free of Melancholy?
Who is not touched more or lesse in habit or disposition? And who is not sick, or ill-disposed, in whom doth
not passion, anger, envie, discontent, fear, and sorrow raigne?"]

C'eravamo tanto amati, as the saying goes – c'eravamo tanto amati, we all loved each other so much. Put it in the
chorus, sing the song, repeat it as often as you like – c'eravamo tanto amati, we all loved each other so much.

Raimondo, pensi per te solamente – pensi per te, Raimondo – solamente. Capisc –

No regrets – or maybe only a few – because there's still an opportunity to attach some faces to them besides
your own.

IMPLICATIONS OF THE LAST HECATOMB

You may not be interested in war, but war is interested in you.
　　　　-Lev Bronshtein, AKA Leon Trotsky

Many of the oldest priests were there, their ceremonial robes
in tatters but the knives they held appeared bright and recently honed.
Most of these men had not been seen in years, having with the passage
of time drifted away without offering any reason for their departure –
singly or in small groups of three or four – retired for good to caves or
small shelters they built themselves in the mountains or along the coastal
plain miles from the temple – worship and ritual now become for them
a private matter, or so many of us had thought. But now here they were
again standing silently in one determined row, facing the gathering crowds.
The animals had not yet been brought towards the altars. Some were
still penned, others tied to trees, and still others were leashed to their handlers.
Current high ranking members of the priestly class went about their preparations
for the sacrifices. Clearly disconcerted by the arrival of their predecessors
in so large a number, they avoided even the slightest acknowledgement
of their presence, though from time to time one of the younger priests could
be seen making furtive glances in their direction – indicative, perhaps,
of the anticipated and inevitably depraved clash between ardent support
and fervent opposition. The masses of people, many from the shantytowns
that had sprung up on the outskirts of the city, quietly pressed forward in order
to catch a better glimpse of the old priests they had not expected to see.
It was taken as no inconsequential omen when a bull broke loose from his
two handlers and charged into the crowd, badly goring one of the worshippers
before it could be subdued. As they hauled the wounded man away, a garland
of red and yellow flowers that had been draped around the bull's neck had
momentarily become entangled in the victim's legs until one of the young priests
stepped forward and hastily pulled it away. In later conflicting recorded versions
of the incident, as well as all the day's events that seemed to stem from it, it was
stated that it had been a child who had been killed by the bull, and in others that
that it had been an old man, a brother of one one of the priests who had returned.
A number of years later in a friend's house I discovered an urn that had been painted
to memorialize the event. The victim rendered in the ceramicist's version of what
happened was a child. But a small fresco in the same house showed him to be an old man.
My host offered no reply when asked about these conflicting representations.

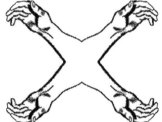

August 27, 2005

BIANCOMANO.
Since he was incapable of judicious thought it was decided that despite his sizeable
debts he owed nothing to anyone – so no one was to be paid and anyone who
complained soon disappeared without a trace – *Justitia Romana*, they said – simply a
matter of business, the way things had always been done when the nature of the debt
called for such *diplomacy* – reasonable, philosophic, and threatening –

AND/OR
You are sweltering and even embarrassed, but nonetheless you provide a sense of antipathy
worth investigating – there's always something kept at arm's length, done so because it
is worth the vantage of this perspective marked at the furthest extent of the palm's
reach, bidding at once to come no further, but also to *go* no further as well – somebody
always wins before the confusion sets in and the process begins again –

IS/OR
What is it about the turned-down corners of pages in a book? Someone else has been
here, that's for damn sure. What was it about these pages – these *particular* pages?
Perhaps an adjustment to the text was being planned – thoughts might have been briefly
entertained to return to them later, maybe add some notes or sharp comments in ink or
pencil to the margins, questioning the writer's judgements or assertions – or perhaps to
come back and underline a favorite or an especially perplexing or annoying word or phrase –

JUDEKKA
Judecca – where the betrayers of benefactors are punished. But where are the benefactors? Where are they
punished? On the fingers of one hand I can count them. One, two, three – no further. And where are the
ungrateful punished? But grace has always been a far more attractive trait than gratitude. Wouldn't you agree?
<*Vexilla regis prodeunt inferni*> – stated thus here not for pretense, but as it was put – <Marching forward under
the flags of the King of Hell, straight at us> says Dante, <*verso di noi; pero dinanzi mira*> – <so keep looking
straight ahead.> Spun out of what Venantus Fortunatus wrote in the sixth century <*Vexilla regis prodeunt*> and
is now sung during Holy Week.

ARROWS, DOTS, AND DASHES [HOMAGE TO ZENO OF ELEA, DIVISER OF PARADOXES]
*The Arrow: Time is made up of instants, which are the smallest measure and indivisible. An arrow is either in motion
or at rest. An arrow cannot move, because for motion to occur, the arrow would have to be in one position at the start of
an instant and at another at the end of the instant. However, this means that the instant is divisible which is impossible
because by definition, instants are indivisible. Hence, the arrow is always at rest.*

Demokritus of Abdera also lodges here, because he ascribed the world to chance –
Reason and reason and reason not the need – only convergence and infinity matter –

Take it. Take it all. That's why it was said. That's why it was put here and allowed to gather amid the silence and dust. A day ahead, a day behind, but never totally losing track. Hot or cold, window open or closed, the room, the hallway, or the street – *Take it. Take it all. That's why it was said. That's why it was put here* If it seems I insist, it's merely a way of striking a balance – of setting both sides of the scale at equal height.

Stylized, awkward, often modishly pagan – whose judgements were these? Probably my own. That too is provided. What of the old priests who had returned, what of Nicolai and his brother, and the unnamed monk who had traveled a great distance from his monastery, probably never to return? And Venantus Fortunatus? Wasn't he Bishop of Poitiers? Hell, man, you know he was. But at what point did his hymn enter the September liturgy? What would the further refinement of this discovery add to the larger matter at hand? Who's asking? Who wants to know? What was it the king of France had right under his nose? It will always be there. A blemish – no, a wart. The same question with the changing answers. All the inessential and superfluous the product of a restless disposition. Scripted on a voluntary basis only. There's a fair measure – and *there* another. And a tone perfectly suited, perfectly adapted, to both – or any. But let us have fewer words and more music. More music to punctuate the silences to come – while Tydeus gnaws on the head of Menalippus. Will Titus be joining us for dinner? I always enjoy watching him wipe the blood and butter from his chin. And will Statius be joining us? Beatrice phoned days ago to say she couldn't come. But perhaps she'll change her mind – and even bring one of her friends. Such women always travel in the company of other women. I know whereof I speak. But you don't have to take my word for it. You need only consult the paintings to see for yourself.

Figaro! Son qua.
Ehi, Figaro! Son qua.

Figaro qua, Figaro la, Figaro qua, Figaro la,
Figaro su, Figaro giu, Figaro su, Figaro giu.

Pronto prontissimo son come il fumine:
sono il factotum della citta.

WITHIN THE NATURE OF A BRUISE

POINTS OF IMPACT

EXIT WOUNDS

MEASURING THE SKULL

A difficult logic for one with plans to pull away –
But not for one who wishes to stay –
Felicita, signora, felicita!

The answer made of everything
But taken from nowhere else –

WALKING AMONG STONES ◆ A HARDENING OF INSTINCTS
Probity metamorphoses into consequence
to establish the precise degree of remorse –
the imagined effort sustained by the corruptions of time

AUGUST 29, 2005

THE ONLY QUESTIONS I REFUSE TO ANSWER ARE WHO, WHAT, AND WHY
No celebrity, no notoriety, no faces staring back, no strange
phonecalls or anonymous communiques, no requests for money
or favors – *no celebrity* – only authority – personal and very private –

As might be expected such an achievement involved more
than a readjustment of paradigms – and would three pages
in either direction have made any difference?

It wasn't a decision so much as an apology for a decision –
for a choice having been made – the specular I, you, he, she,
they, and it all combining in contentious ceremony –

This going about from place to place though never traveling far,
this going *about it*, this finding, this taking, this naming and
renaming, this placing and misplacing, this abandoning –

Where's the rest, not the addendum to the addenda, where's the rest
that remains when the calm returns to such clarity with an illusion
of renewed purpose? *Where?* Is it there in your hand? On your tongue?

IN THE ROOK'S MOUTH
"The obstacles, the tropes – there are some, there are others, there are *enough* – so let's move on to other
unrelated matters, or make a virtue of the parapetetic." [He was trying to learn how to live by listening to songs
and going to movies. But, unlike with philosophy, literature, and religion when put to the same use, he was
seriously limiting the possible range of what might be held culpable for guiding his actions – or so he was told,
appropriately enough, by another moviegoer whistling in the wind a tune he wasn't sure perhaps he hadn't
heard before.]

LARGE EYES, SMALL HANDS, SHARP TEETH
When a page of handwritten notes is crumpled the dog comes to the desk seeking to shred it further – *inérudit*
and above sea level – marking with customary dexterity an over involvement with the ambiguous and the *soi
disant* mitigations of marginality, that in other contexts might allow for a more decisive analysis – one suggests,
one argues, another assumes, another interprets, another detects, one subverts, one contrives, another
urgently notes, another calmly acquiesces, and one concurs, and still another takes up a further set of phonetic
proximities also misheard in the first instance –

ARENA [*L. HARENA*, PLACE OF SAND, PLACE OF BATTLE]
This is how bad it is, or, as she would have me think how bad I'd made it – a rebuke with varying shades of
intensity is posited in every response she makes to any questions I ask – no matter how casually put – as though
whatever information I might seek, even regarding her health, was exploitive and meant to take from her
something she was now, after more than thirty years, unwilling to provide.

ANTICIPATES – BUT ALSO UNMISTAKABLY ECHOES [HOW IS THIS POSSIBLE]
"We're probably looking for a tall woman, at least 6 foot, size 14 dress, size 10 shoe. But this doesn't answer our question 'Who killed Brooke?' Our tall woman is only, shall we say, a 'person of interest' at the moment – unless we assume being tall and a woman are sufficient reasons to ascribe motives for committing a violent crime of this sort – no robbery involved – at least as far as has been determined – we have no idea where the deceased lived. There was saltwater in the victim's lungs, but his clothes were bone dry, an icepick wound behind the right ear, two broken teeth, a page of music in one of his jacket pockets, and a coin found on his tongue."

A FANLIGHT OF STAINED GLASS

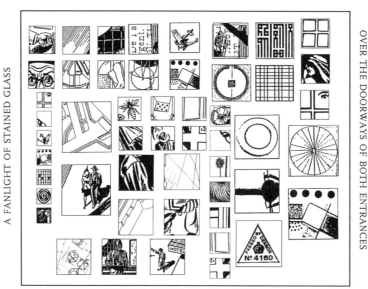

OVER THE DOORWAYS OF BOTH ENTRANCES

ANOTHER STORY ABOUT A STORY

Saying precisely the same thing –
There is no exact equivalent without cumbersome periphrasis –
Something is obviously lost--or has been missing all along –

Q. Nevermind the set-ups and digressions. What really happened?
A. Set-ups and digressions.

When *this* was said *that* was meant and when *that other*
Was said *this other* was meant – coded language and
Circumstantial evidence = Doubt.

ANOTHER USE FOR THUNDER
　　　　　Afterwards, if it's springtime,
And there's been sufficient thunder to bring them on,
Truffles appear. 'Ah, Africa!' cries the gourmet,
'You can keep your grain-supply, unyoke your oxen,
so long as you send us truffles!'
　　　　　　　—Juvenal, Satire V, l. 118-122

A LONG POSTPONED VENGEANCE

AND ALLOWED LIFE TO GO ON

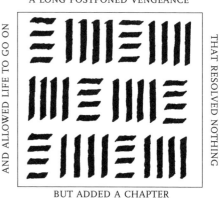

THAT RESOLVED NOTHING

BUT ADDED A CHAPTER

August 31, 2005

Anecdotal evidence, isolated thunderstorms, half-disguised interests, flooding in coastal areas, 20/20 x 20/20, a master of the parapetetic piss – bladder empty – trousers dry – shoes unscathed – a rare talent mastered late in youth, but before which came marking corners with a stick – sharp angles – not words – cut in the sand, night echoes – the purest idiom, an alien place – an entire continent, what else might be determined – the proviso being complex and alimentary, a book for my brother – you have no brother, a book for my sister – you want no sister, a book for my father – you know no father, a book for my mother – you had no mother, voracious odors, sawdust on the floor, the plenary and the viatic taken together – although neither spiritual nor intellectual depth increases now that these have been attained, feigned gratitude, distracted motions, erasures, deviations, annulments interposed, repeated use of the obelus, adages configured, knife-to-knife repartee, recitations packed in straw, stillness – trope to trope, the last page for the last day, one color into another – not by means of light but by means of light's mathematics, fabled antipathies, breath first – or look for the answer – which is it – some never need ask, running the edges of Numa's ancile – the course, ∞ encrypted – its own space resourcefully corrupted by the smoke from Ixion's wheel, something else will be *cured* in this smoke, heat and dust add texture to the chrism, marble pastures, broken glass, pieces of the torn page – their distribution only a palimpsest not a puzzle, 'E' tattooed on the Ledaean body, the same as the 'E' inscribed at Delphi – Rabelais yawns, Montaigne nods – others perpetually out of the sun ask *Who*, tragedy or farce – one word more or less determines both within the events recounted – though more are suspect than remain viable, solitude – solace – and scorn, rolling a dead lion into a hole, vigilant – provided it doesn't make silence part of the transaction, a clout of flesh over the cock and balls – suggesting an ascetic might emerge from the navel like Athena from the mungo and promiscuous head of Zeus, here a vindictive compassion enters the line of reasoning following the paths winding through the olive groves, contractile equivalents – none are contrite in the poses they strike – an interpretation of the living flesh – for dollars – wine and bread and butter – but meatless as the sanctions of a forgotten Friday, no license to be gained by repudiation, and none ever by bearing witness, any who arrive now or in the future and wish to know more are like the corroboration they seek – merely the consequence of deletion, no explanations offered where none are called for, a new page provided for the last day, anabasis bearing the strain of certain applications –

LACRIME D'INCHIOSTRO ROSSO
C'era un uomo,
Mal'occhio tenevo.
Passò un nostro caro amico
Con palma d'oliva in mano.
L'acqua fece seccare,
L'erba fece malagnare,
A quattro cantoni spumicava.

mules at the wake

HOMO FABER

this then
then this

that then

ne pas ecrire À LA SUITE

—Valéry

July 11, 2006:

XX-eye / XX-I

In copia minor error [In excess there lies less danger of error].

. . . as it was reckoned in those archaic times.

The written word preserved
as a confidential archive to be
consulted in times of uncertainty –

. . . pseudonymous versions of frenzied utterance.

Particular occasions
Particular individuals

Well-phantoms echoing outward – a hoard of spasms.

The pebbled lens still in place
Frying his liver in the broadest daylight –
Higher noon by a Friday week.

Stretches in prospect extorted in prospect –
Mansions on the horizon cut by the cang.

All the dead turning their absence into love.

Subito convulses *subito* –
Christ have mercy under us
Lord have mercy under us.

Baited in abatement the only decorum . . .

Immune to the afflictive genesis . . .

You come and go as you please. How many of you are there?

Hieroglyph or interrogative trope?

Axlegyre

JULY 12, 2006:

'neither consonant unto reason, nor correspondent unto experiment'
—Thomas Browne

Wisest no better – squandered in vigilance

Rubbing the focus into aim

Ribboned from the distaff –
Imago the half-task –
Liminal-forsaken –
Tocsin-thithered –
Faceless succor

Not fragment but multicolored ranging decimal devising reason

Dulled by 'Yes'
Stemmed by 'No'

Apathy and premonition

Plumbline to pallet
Coffer to gat

A fragility as sterile as poison

[doaty, tacot, matinal, erythrite, rapparee, rafflesia, signaculum, plagal, nautch,
limae, poisers, xanthic, mammae, scutal, gantelope, pucking, areca, mard, cere,
pentade, bascule, cernèd, clonic, latibule, vomer, chlorotic, frôleur, cavaletto,
ganzy, strom, vire]

10 days bled –
Against a pillow of light –

Its tentative reach
From grassy nape to weedy pubis –

Tempered by deceit and mechanical gestures of solace –

Axlegyre sans arghile –

July 13, 2006:

Rubrics and residua –

Explicit only in faceted coherence –

Not a logic of events and expectation –

The course of action erupts
Beyond immediate lexicon or valorized syntax

Sometimes courage, sometimes affection – what then remains?

Unresolved by retinal thought –
Anticipation is a function of both imminence and repose –

[MEMORY] One path ran along the clay from the broken door to a silver maple,
And from there to the pond that stretched from a small dirt road
To the first rise against the eastern horizon. [CHOSEN]

A keening strobe runs across all that's left –
Grafting contraptions and patience with lightning
Differences and opacities, similarities and complications,
The eventual bracketed by shreds of the ungoverned and matter-of-fact.
Persuasion follows and enviable convictions unique to you,
Now ruminant now decisive now progress and determined finagle
Accurate until it comes to rest.

Not West – just not far enough East –

Seed imitates seed –

Intonations – Displacement – Preemption – Weird hybrids

CONTRA PYTHAGORAS
Prediction is very difficult, especially about the past.

JULY 14, 2006:

Too polite to listen
Too rude to hear

A mouse theater covered in ivy – what the Georgics demanded –

Bric-a-brac, paper hats, whiskey, and deacons –

The fundamental slackness that reveals repeated effort –

The direction made – but not yet taken –

The technique, the work, the will
Sped-up – and blocked –

Urged, half-meant, the argument –

A congruent din undeduced –

Idle heights – eroded into spectrum –
The next world is exhausted
We hear so much
Various in discovery and breathlessly joined to exclusion –

The barbed lurch
the consequent parts
include isolation –

"I am tomorrow," and my fault is mortal.

Parabolic in perspective
From margin to back page
Exact words into furthermore –

Cause *schmerz* and effect *kommerz* –

Speculative *and* black and white –

And [in] And [with] And [however]

JULY 15, 2006:

polyphloisboio among these rocks –

Moon-blackened tides –

Must not forget the part intended for conclusion –
The widening angle of

Full, fair, and particular –
all for speculation –

Aegri Ephemeris

Preliminary findings suggest a variety of terms
everso saeclo [the torn word], rendition, bang and burn –

Excavation to a deeper stratum not accommodated –

The *are* not the *what* –
circumspect and not particularly informative, as usual –

"Tell me things – but not about your life. And I'll give
the matter some thought. I'm looking for a place to go –
but starting out from a place I've never been. How about it?
What might you say? What might you offer that might
determine where I might journey? Give yourself a moment.
These things occasionally take a bit of time – if not necessarily
deep thinking. Also, avoid indignation – or showing any –
that might appear to stem from my request. In the end it
will serve little or no purpose in advancing your cause.
Whatever that might be. As I recall, you came to me with a
proposition of some sort having, or so it seemed, poked me in
the ribs to gain my attention. Don't spare the details – but avoid
any inclination toward chronicle. In medias res is perfectly all right.
It worked for most of the ancients and those who came immediately
after and learned their tricks from them. Keep commentary to a
minimum. But I want to be able to follow – closely if necessary.
But not too close, because it will prevent the achievement of a true
sense of perspective. One might take this suggestion to heart in
all such matters. Don't be ashamed of your eyes, let them, not your
tongue, shape what you provide for me. No speaking in tongues.
It might be useful – even preferable – if I start you off with something
brief but dense. I'll begin then by jabbing an elbow in your ribs."

1. anonominative
2. harmonyms
3. crawligraphy
4. alcocolic
5. renaissource
6. sodgestive
7. emotikon
8. cartwhores
9. radiocean
10. enveloaf
11. serveil
12. imitorsion
13. gratiturd
14. faundull
15. situaction
16. audibubble
17. wormwould
18. racketicketer
19. narraturf
20. comprehinder
21. engolf
22. cornsitter
23. benefiddle
24. terminoloquy
25. lunaticycle
26. elimiluminate
27. blackmoile
28. improversion
29. eventualibi
30. interpretorsion
31. nervice
32. piguptrek/biguptrek/piguptrick/biguptrick
33. fernychore
34. yesdearday
35. knoticaul
36. limoushine
37. porkypine
38. neolurkism
39. preditort
40. nocturinal
41. reminiscience
42. obscare
43. glimmore
44. mordon't
45. menopaws
46. humdumb
47. errortic
48. dialock
49. investipurgative
50. ignorank/ignorink
51. fewdual
52. predescissors
53. serialibi
54. suspiscion
55. vividiot
56. accountrue
57. inadequark
58. curiouseful/curiouseless
59. retiscents
60. wrecommind

July 17, 2006:

Cinq à sept —

Solo vivit in illa.
Sola vivit in illo.

The sole function of origin is to recede —
But at an angle —

kalpa = 4.32 billion years
worked the black ink to gray

Strabo reports that in 20 BCE, a yogi who was part
of an Indian embassy visiting Caesar Augustus in Rome
burnt himself to death in an act of self-immolation.

Centripetal, centrifugal marginalia
unanxious in the memory —

What's variously textured here is the tendency to self-question
and the querulousness that often succeeds wonder —

Staggered in the interest of trembling shadows —
Trembled in the interest of staggering shadows —
A dilated perturbation of debauched chiaroscuro

A blue and white faience stove stood in a corner of the largest
downstairs room. It was of such a size to heat the entire house.

Purling: The motion of a small stream running among obstructions;
also, the sound it makes in doing so.

— Pythagorhythm —

What trace lingers in the edit?

Perhaps the bricks, wood, and plaster had long ago soaked it up.
But something's on the loose. People are seeing and hearing things.

July 18, 2006:

Wet ink drying on the eyelids –
Ensorcelled mazes
Minimal insight plethoral possibility
A catalogue of the haphazard and abortive
Radical trajectories
A capacity for mutation at cross-purposes
The path of the misanthrope and panther

Et similia plurima – and many similar things
parting the frayed edge into threads –

I'd like a supply of pencils made of shami – acacia suma –
a wood reputed to contain fire and therefore used to kindle sacrificial fires –

I stayed in the sun. I said things. I made plans, and wore dark glasses.

Yes is anything else, unobserved.

Ankle, angle, à clef –

An ebb runs in the ditch purling through the fingers –

Of the not to the not from the not –
pulse to pallor –
no effect but complement and anxious surmise –
a hunted thought from the footsore

Nearer to the next nearest to the last –
Dante's last quarter mile – step step step
andante step step step step
presto step step step step step

CARTOUCHE
Clawlines to modesty reckon the savvy –
Egyptian geometry maintained in Roman numerals

Let it begin on page 1 – if page 3
the questions will remain: what has been taken away?
what has been replaced?

JULY 19, 2006:

Vahana = ursus

Late = in time to be out of place –

Chromatic resolve –
subscription to the socially acceptable is right off –

No trace of love in the panic to solace –

With suicide bombing
proportionality is taken out of the equation –

What's needed is a mathematics outside the quantitative.

Radicalism is always a matter of degree, except for those opposing it.

TO DO TODAY
Park the truck
Round them up
Load them in
Haul them away

MATCH BOX BLUES
I'm settin here wonderin' would a matchbox hold my clothes
I'm settin' here wonderin' would a matchbox hold my clothes
I ain't got so many matches but I got so far to go
1. The world is everything that fits in the case.
2. What is in the case, in fact, is the extent of adamic facts.
3. The logical picture of the facts is the though.
4. The though is the significant prop.
5. Props are tooth-functions of alimentary props.
(An alimentary prop is a tooth-function of itself.)
Etc

"We are so estranged from our human essence that the direct language of man,
the expression of need, strikes us as an offense against the dignity of man."
   —Karl Marx, *Early Writings*

"Good-nature is that benevolent and amiable temper of mind which disposes us
to feel the misfortunes, and enjoy the happiness of others; and consequently
pushes us on to promote the latter, and prevent the former; and that without any
abstract contemplation on the beauty of virtue, and without the allurements or
terrors of religion."
   —Henry Fielding, *Essay on the Knowledge of the Characters of Men*

Put it here, think of it later, abandon it again –

Constrained to produce, to reveal distinct features,
to argue from proximity, to suggest the elusive or
expedient from little or nothing –

The end of the day, the end of the page, the ends in themselves –

Thin broth small spoon –

An ominous dream described, then retold with added detail,
and then enlarged and highly embellished, for 3 different strangers –

Decipherment is invariably descriptive the more philosophic its original terms –

The burden of what has been taken away –

No allegories, only shadow play –

Elder is a tree of ill-omen, and countrymen
used to raise their caps to it as they walked past.
A tree of shame, it was used for hanging criminals.

I like quiet places, but they always make me feel
I should hurry whatever I've come there to do.

MEMORIES OF SPOOK ROCK ROAD
Shrapnel
and blowing leaves

JULY 21, 2006:

Once a flâneur – though no longer nimble or lively
but still *eager* – always a flâneur –

On the rue de la Femme-sans-Tête
a large room illuminated only at one end –

Serenity impeding density amends recollection –

Once knew – in prefernce to yet to know, have yet to say –

Extricate and balance the message from the message and conclusion –

A raw veneer –

The carelessly hidden balanced
along a low narrow arc fraying to accompany –

Silent feed-lines of copper and brass catch the light
along a corridor flanked with polished instruments
keys levers dials knobs pipes and at carefully determined intervals
dignified raised ceramic numbers coded green and black –
lead conduits for run-off and waste are hidden in the walls and beneath the floors –

Mnemonic clamor –
A word, a phrase in a carnival alphabet
waiting to be set to music –

The prosecution advances its atonal welcome
The only way to be decisive is to be slow and quiet
Like a fist closing – the only way to b e slow and quiet is to be quick –

Use, usury, 'usered' –

RHYTHMS OF 3
[*Won*] Fugitive, fatal, and still further on –
[*Due*] Not mortal enough – but ambient, eponymous, and furtive –
[*Tree*] Shapely, though neither young nor beautiful,
but frugal, impatient, and uncompromising –

"I remember nothing that happened worth relating this day. How many such days
does mortal man pass!" -James Boswell, *Journal*, July 21, 1763

JULY 22, 2006:

ORCHÉSOGRAPHIE – PROBOULEUSIS

"the falsetto of reason"   —Beckett

Pas seuls pas seuls pas seuls
Time stands still, selectively
– A whistle sounds

Distracted intimacy, incongruous proximity,
divisions, cunning, and euphoria

Zero – *obtained*
Nails added later

The minima is limit – but diffuse

Something seen many times but named only once –

Diminished by enumeration –
Mitigated by the unavoidable affirmation of sound

An isolated entry that must be surrounded
by more isolated entries in order to function –

A random pretext = an excursion *to* –
Distilled and dilated

The angle the horizon makes with the corners of the eyes and the next idea
– Conviction – with all the authority of the timeproof colloquial

RAVAGED POINTILLIST
Small loads, bitter novelties

INLAND AREAS
A normal day, 110° in Sparta

THUMB SAP
Gums the trigger, tangles the hammer

THE REVENGE OF THE MODERATE
A greasy peony between the teeth

JULY 23, 2006:

PREFERENCES OF THE BOWER BIRD

Among corrective patterns and attached systems
is the desire to question all prior assumptions
and those promised perfections cheated by strange symbols.
Can such things be said in a manner such as this –
seeing the empty speech balloon weighing down
on the speaker's head like a misshapen piece of ice
placed there by some offending sorrow.
An intelligent futility comes up with a compromise,
as is customary when need extols desire,
and offers a grudging acceptance of odd alliances.
What is still missing is a sense of timeless calm –
but there is always the next word and the possibilities
predicated more on the awareness than on the consequent idea.
Passion bypasses contentment if only to be better remembered.
We know it casts a shadow but that's as close as we can get.

        *   *   *

How much of the mongrel and rudimentary sustains the reaches of origin?

A tight-lipped antipathy accounts for the ventriloquism.

The subjectivity behind intuition is immune to correction and logical violation.

The translated object handmade,
its gravitational identity worked through spectra
reveals a stamina of subtractive means –

Appropriate the logical from the optical to unmask the link.

Beautiful, pious, graceful, and immodest –

It's not a matter of putting 2 and 2 together but of separating 2 from 3, 4, or 5 –
or more likely 2 from 2.

July 24, 2006:

Major instances of corruption in the text have been adduced. Despite the attestations of purported eye-witnesses and the corroboration of the earliest printers, inconsistencies abound. Had the judge arranged for the block and axe to be ready at dawn or had this service been provided by the executioner who considered it part of his responsibilities and, being a man known to rise late, set the performance of his duties to take place at noon instead of at first light?

The document in hand has come down to us after at least two stages of transmission: the first done in the hand of a fastidious but somewhat idiosyncratic copyist, and the other through the typesetting-work of an elderly compositor – a man possessing a reputation for unreliable workmanship due to his love of drink.

There is a remarkable spareness to both texts that coincides with the setting of the events they narrate – described simply as 'an uninhabited island'. Sufficient space was left for the names of the characters involved but it had been left blank in both versions, and its actual scope suggested only by two small decorative elements of the compositor's choosing.

The emblems employed by the compositor were meant to represent the ornaments drawn by the original copyist. But they did so only in their placement. In no way did they replicate what the copyist had indicated. The compositor had replaced a carefully drawn hand and a woman's face in profile with an animal horn and a pair of mason's calipers.

It was the known custom to allow an hour's interval to elapse between the time of execution and the official pronouncement of death. the compositor's version ignores the annotation to this effect placed by the copyist in the margin opposite the passage pertaining to the block and axe.

Among other discrepancies are the use of apostrophes to signify colloquial ellipses, as well as inflections and elisions in the copyist's version; these have been omitted entirely from that of the compositor and replaced with a liberal use of brackets, hyphens, and the breaking of long lines for the purpose of 'justification'.

The theory that the copyist's version had passed through the hands of an unidentified reviser before coming to the compositor still remains to be satisfactorily refuted. Another theory suggests that these anomalies were intended by the text's author who, it has been speculated, supervised the work of both the copyist and compositor.

JULY 25, 2006:

Among the squinting, sweating, scowling, stylish, and scantily clad –
The horizontal has its uses, the vertical has its appeal.[1]

Moral grief has become the focus of fragmented rumination
It cuts the distance to the Law
Seeks revenge – [2]

Doing the same thing over and over
and expecting different results
is one definition of insanity –
Doing the same thing over and over
and being pleased with the same results is another – [3]

[Written over the course of the day (with other elements omitted here
intervening) I can see how these 4 pieces of writing might be related, flowing
from one to the other and, at the same time, by being brought together on the
page realize the fulfillment of the idea stated in the first fragment. What accretive
pressures accommodate 'unity' once the disparate is initiated? And is such
self-reflexive observation purely the result of isolation? But what might further
coalesce around the final word in the 3rd fragment?][4]

Much of this seems to be in anticipation of something not yet fully definable.
These brief passages are either at the heart of certain yet unnamed issues or
shaping their edges. I can't determine which at this point.

– Parallel *or* reflect?

"What's this? The same knife used to cut the bread that was used first to carve
the bloody roast?"

"Spontaneously, from the poetry of the unforeseen, there arises a philosophy of
the absurd."   —René Pomeau

Solitude is meant for exploration – not captivity or valueless isolation.

What quiet is –

At an angle to the music
The ink-deep thin edge of the wedge

Silence isolates and particularizes. Sound homogenizes. Silence, however, is not
merely an absence of sound. It is rather a distillation of sound. Silence enhances
the feedback of other sensations, enabling access to imaginative contexts that
only ambiguity provides.

– She would replenish the table stakes by spending an hour or two on the street, return with a mix of French and American money, play for an hour, and then head back to the street. She obviously never wandered far, returning, as I said, in an hour or so to reclaim her cards and usual place at the table.

The mask demands –

The neglected perpetuates--not what is taken in turn.

Quarter tone progression achieved by added frets and the bending of strings –
i.e. punctuation, italics, spelling, and phrase structure –

The shape throughout, day by day, is that of the net –

Grasped and tangled by the cords of a written space
turned straight to the naked edge that lures but doesn't cut
A cold and shaken slouch pulls the web tighter
against the breath's harmonic ply

The icon of analogy struck out of certain verbs
Names the knot at the source hidden in the quibble
Tangle to tangle its reach over the light to the crease
turns in its commerce what the balance cannot validate
The fold in the formula a record of intuitive endeavors
serendipitous at the graft – their practiced options
isolated in ascribed motive replicate a straw grid
against the letterings of another prediction
Syncopated vertigo gauges the alternatives the prank and debt intend

These glosses in omination – all such graphing invokes the net –

Activity circumscribed by task indifferent to progression –
A prolific quotidian become a tantrum of speculation –

Blank legacy for the mark –
like a rebus-strewn affection
of uncertaine resemblance and
'no speciall place of beginning nor end'

The fold in the formula turned in its commerce
that balance cannot validtae

Hearing the tine echoing fragile in the g's

JULY 27, 2006:

the surrender of the whole to detail
imminence enhanced by chaos

farraginous sleep – with variora
chiaro[topos]scuro

poise, conflict, subsidence –
shallow stones begin to drift and reshape the path

a new way, not an old way – or another way
more thorough, less rosy

seeing 'all', feeling 'some', describing 'any'
seeing 'some', feeling 'any', describing 'all'
seeing 'any', feeling 'all', describing 'some'

Distances and angles
proximity to distance from
steeple tree pillar wall standing figure
navigating through a staggering array of choices
boulevard to avenue and street
looking backward toward the horizon

*The many nonsensical things which he says to himself are the consequence of his
monologue style of conversation. He is alone, he gets bored, he must speak. He says
something reasonable, he cannot develop it any further, something else comes into his
head, and then that is repressed and erased by a third and fourth thought, one right
after the next. A terrible confusion then ensues, he becomes moody, he talks nonsense
and chatters words without meaning as his mind subsides again. When he comes
into contact with people, he believes that he must be gracious and sociable, so he asks
questions, says something, but without any interest in either the stranger or what the
stranger says to him. He becomes so tangled up in himself in the meantime that he
annuls the second person and speaks to himself. If he finds himself in the embarassing
situation of having to answer, it is unlikely that he would think that he had not
understood the question because he does not pay any attention at all, and so he cuts off
the visitor with nonsense.* -Wilhelm Waiblinger

The prehistory of mimetic rationality
turns the single loop echo – hits the language wall
makes an inscription

Their predictions pertained to unfinished business –
something to do with memory and coaxing enchantment
from a different face. Any face.

July 28, 2006:

THE MOSAIC VIRUS
[1] The most important rule was the one I broke first.
[2] To be read not in the wrong way but in many wrong ways –
[3] Won, paid, and forgotten – lost, paid, and remembered.
[4] Dreams mix with memories creating doubt.
[5] Curiosity – curiosity and benevolence –
[6] It's money that ruins us – that and bad timing.
[7] Of the rest all that remains is a disturbing aptitude . . .
[8] Not the object but the marks it bears –
[9] Nothing comes from the light that wasn't first in darkness.
[10] What are they after, these people retracing their steps?

ACOUSTIC STRUCTURES
Left ear over right eye
Right ear across left ear over left eye

CARTA
The river the wet thread –

ZOËPOEM
Some handfuls larger than others

THE SPITTEN BOOK
'For Erthe I Am'

GOLIARDIC ADMIXTURE
Mon pote
Über jeden Tadel erhaben

LEAVES OF GRASS LEAVES OF HYPNOS
Kafka's snow, smelling peonies, telephoning

THE DARKENING GLARE
Emptying the distance

SONG
One word at a time of one word in time
One word at a time of one word *intime*

BURIED IN THE GARDEN
Where everything is

JULY 29, 2006:

SABBATH GENTRY
As these things go – between the iris and the sphinx –
one day more or less, despite the lateness of the season –
one of you stays behind.

HIDDEN IN THE FLOWERS
Ticking sleuth and yodeling sherpa
tête-bêche

BAKED SHIRT
        Hence the problem of pots. —Jacques Lacan
Sylvan historian
I placed a jar in Tennessee
Say, Pot, pot
'Jug Jug' to dirty ears

GRAVITY
The only alternative trajectory
of the last word restored

WINDOWED ARC/IMPERFECT RESOLUTION
From and fro

APPROACHING INVISIBILITY
Eye marking
the barbed perfection of 3

STRAITS OF CAPRICE
The most severe sense of history
the one associated with pleasure

A SOLITARY MAN
Old gods of the loopy nocturne
  Pouring coffee at midnight –
Between her sword and her spoon
  Whose muddy shoes?

ŒUVRES COMPLÈTES
Prehistory (no limit), mound builders,
pitiless interim, meddling rigor,
hooligans and harridans, lingerie indigence

July 30, 2006:

It's a Sunday afternoon with Highwire Nebucho
Symboliste et Metallurgiste come around with his hats in hand.
Like Mungo Park he has travelled along a dry stony height covered with mimosas,
His barely discernible modesty no worse than gratitude mistaken for grace,
Or his spoken accomplishment of a mechanical device fashioned out of
Pieces of wood, plaster, strips of cloth, and braided horsehair –

LISTS OF WORDS, FORMS, AND PHRASES COMPILED IN CANONICAL SERIES
Elephantine [FIRST CATARACT] Semna [SECOND CATARACT]
Tombos [THIRD CATARACT] beyond Nuri [FOURTH CATARACT]
[FIFTH CATARACT] Meroë beyond [SIXTH CATARACT] Naga to the East

UPSUD/UP-L'EST/UPNORD/UP-L'OUEST
Two red squares situated to the right on the vertical
One precisely above the other
Each measuring 1 $1/4$″ on the diagonal and
Separated by a narrow band of cream-colored paper
From the left a thick black line three inches long
Extends to within $1/2$″ of the base of the bottom red square
Beneath the black line and just beyond its middle point
Are two small red dots juxtaposed $1/16$″ apart
a series of small circles, dashes, curved and jagged lines
are configured to the right and left beneath the dots

SO DENSE THE SPACE AROUND IT NEVER FORMED
The objective case used throughout these pages

ARTICULATED RISE
Hook and nail detached

TEXT
There is no erosion of confidence when lines form –
records have been kept since the third century

RUSE DE GUERRE
An indispensible role in the organization of discourse

THE VOICE OF THOUGHT
No words

JULY 31, 2006:

A nick out of the hard frost
starts the collapse –

MODEL OF VINDICATION
I never caught up, not with what needed
to be said, but with what was omitted

An interventionist understanding of language's [onomastic] relation to nature –
(Rahu the dragon is the cause of eclipses)

THE LESSER DISTINCTION
kekoimemenon (those who were asleep)
koimomenois (them that sleep)
not identified in any way beyond the vague term 'many'

It wasn't the only question, but all the others seemed to require the same answer –

INTERSUBJECTIVE POLYPHONY
An amended recollection, an opportunity to extricate an allusion from the unruly
quiet, the rude song of the proven – call it what you will – it was a topic worthy
of an estimate. We had put our trust in him not only because his sack was the
largest but also because of the way he wrestled with it, shifting it from shoulder
to shoulder or dragging it along the ground for miles when it was necessary to
do so. Besides he had been the first to speak. It was night, there was fog, the
sack was of a prodigious size. There is no need to tell me now that these factors
all contributed to obvious errors in judgement. I don't think I could hear you
if you did. People are always telling me things. I don't wish to have anything
handed to me and would prefer to remain here, sitting with legs crossed, arms
at rest and palms up in this close circular space surrounded by young saplings,
flowers, bushes, and weeds. Just place at my feet whatever it is you think requires
my attention, and if it doesn't explode or blow away in the wind, sooner or later,
maybe while you're discovering the hint of limestone in the wine, I'll get around
to picking it up.

Concentrate your attention on a single object: a tooth, a piece of bone, an emerald
wrapped in a page of newsprint.

TESTIMONY, GNARLED MARGINS, CHAGRIN, MANDARIN DETACHMENT
The chances of our reaching the banks of the river some 10 kilometers distant
were further impeded by the stones of a tower that had collapsed and now
formed part of a wall that extended as far as the eye could see between us and
the forest path we knew to be just beyond. Who had built the wall from the fallen
tower no one could say. Nor was there anyone who could tell us whether once we
reached the river our preferred direction should be upstream or downstream.

ascoso

[HERMETIC ANONYMITY]

e l'infinita vanità del tutto

—Giacomo Leopardi, *Canti*

la più ascosa / e più riposta via prendono ad arte

—Tasso

There's nothing here to be measured –
simply take your share. Pensa, lettor.
The rift in perspective – a record of intuitive endeavors
serendipitous at the graft – limned by the eye.
Blood on the chain, a form of motion
written in black and blue, the body means to go back.
Verticals stagger and extend the spiral –
resisting the pull of gravity, slicing
a disputed form into gestures. Said –
to be – said to be, seen. Said *to be*.
Argot, hieroglyphics, and the play of appearances,
micromass of all sorts. Tilt of lens,
shape and angle of mirror, light caught in the bevel
from the torch of Phlegyas. Prenda, lettor.
Né, per lo foco, in là più m'appressai.
The flight of ideas as from a rookery –
elusive and incalculable, to test memory
with all that is aloud. Whiteness opportunes
a geometry, blackness contact –
as the visible dilates on the seeable,
thinned to the consequent expansion of thought.
More work for Megaera, shaping every context--
eêroeis, dira dira, dira.
The smoke rises, catching a breeze as it parses the birds.
Expectation determines the path of their trajectory,
like an endless exchange of retractions.
A falsetto saved for urgency – its declamatory purpose
elastic enough to allow dozens of provisional tunes
to step out onto the rough boards and square stones.
Enunciation into the graphing matrix, tropic
to latitude, parable, discursion, and arck.
Prophetic clarity arrived at between *not yet* and *no longer*.
Variable asides plumb by allusion any baedekered elliptic,
imponderable contradictions hidden in no optic shadow –
only questions can follow the situation that silence enjoys.

7/27/06 – 8/1/06

Broken stories – tales of the clamp –
a mouthful of sugar spit out for a mouthful of salt.
The path multiplies the division,
the steps taken are its algebraic resolve,
to end, ever in a further premonition.
Bones ground to a fine powder and dissolved in wine –
to gather some necessity out of the averages,
not perfection nor accuracy but the reach
of both within the attitude of terms.
When they finished their meal they arranged
the remaining bones in specific patterns
across the bottom and along the sides of a shallow pit
that had been dug by one of them who had earlier
been chosen by lot. The hole was then carefully
filled with dirt and leaves so as not to disturb
the arrangement of bones. The top layer of earth
was strewn with small branches, stones, and acorns.
The memory that resists change and the one that yields –
not to change – but to the agency of a further memory –
the immutable and plaintive combine to give
a philosophic emphasis to what is still unknown –
the charmed inertia of the middle distance.
Metamorphosis realized in terms of detachment
emerges only in contradiction – regret, nostalgia,
or loss become a gesture for that limit.
To *enter* is to *overtake* – the words written by hand –
pages where the stillness is constructed
and the geography never immediate –
abandoned to the darkness it lifts
grained by the coin's milled edge.
Uncertainties better expressed by music than
attempts at the ever-deferred constancy of the foregone
mistaken for principled initiative.
Value emerges from the limitations placed on the arbitrary,
further obviated by what is thought to be transcendent –
the intuitive exploited beyond the normative frames
of classical strategies, neither arrangements or situations,
the future forever a measure of the past.
Accord sounds in the ears, a prediction of what might
comprise the interim until the behest earns its predicate.

Adhesion both to hide and fill –
synaptic from crypt to crypt
without the prepared figure, competent plausibility,
passage, omen, deposition, pastoral sense, coinage,
pivots, muted cataract, sediment, conjecture,
composure, parlance – persistence never implemented.
mirrors beyond the limits of inquiry –
where inquiry raises an image looming behind the light,
no more a shadow than a closer look.
Torsion unravels and becomes an improvisation of the tempered.
You performed as one who goes in darkness,
Carrying the light behind him, not profiting himself,
But of use to those who follow.
Antecedent and conveyance, a rhythm outside recurrence,
yet still in the service of ritual, the impress of print,
anything persistent, anything taut – reckoning –
motion without the 'E' – put in the world –
obeying a distance passing unfamiliar
while the damp light pulls away – extenuated by the sun.

8/2/06

Rufous-tipped – strong, yellowish pink, to moderate orange –
the token bestowed, off-spindle, bearing gifts, ardent footwork,
feverish debate, and diatribe. Neon falls from the air. The quick
are found with the crimped and eluded. Tents folded, hands out.
Yawn-rebukes are conjugated amid a shower of fractured tiles,
splintered glass, and shattered timbers. Speeded-up, slowed-down,
speeded-up – down, around, and over. Rooms, walls, like parts of
speech, fall away. Some run towards the alluvial flames in a triangulation
determined by ganglion, lard, and carotid pigment.
What disappears will not budge. Progress traces
an indiscriminate edge – any remainder is manipulated by
complicated dictation into document, assessment, and misgivings.
What remain are the repletions of a tunnel awaiting an entrance,
its adjacent heap readily confused with a wall or door.
The exponential moves quickly, the story too big to live in the head.
Faint voices, daily alarms, attentive ears all trying to intercept the future.
The dialect you hear depends on which side of the river you are standing.
Illusion – the invariable hedge against catastrophe – defers to
legends of the morgue unburdened through rectangular gratings.
Amid the familiar creak and whine thrown on the wind
no all clear sounds from the gypsum works.

8/3 – 4/06

A distinction should be made between what has been lost and
what must be surrendered. The same would apply to what has been
left behind and what through oversight had not been burned. One might
reason that their proud manufacture alone contributed to the variance.
Flames, barbed wire, muted music, and snow – the humorless urgency of
the misappropriated something preferred to the appropriate nothing.
In a less than intact arena of mental effort the retrospective
viewing of charismatic patterns has given way to resolve's
crusted fingers scraping away at the next bourne of the nod.
A city of fires, ringing pavements, and collapsing houses,
as well as poets reciting their poems in August.
The conversion that flight leaves unfulfilled –
the immutable negated by a sense of self-preservation
outruns the audible and anything heated by the sun.
A climbing shadow fulfills a gesture, one hand held up with
palm turned inward, the other hand passing up and down along it.
The parrots of Sparta would offer an interpretation.

8/4/06

By definition, by deduction, by refinement – if one
of the conditions is violated it cannot be extended except
intuitively. Where nothing will be, someone is. Left in place.
Held loosely by thought, held fast by idea.
Without guide or precedent the self-controlled observer
supplies the segments with an ordinal number.
The conversion that flight leaves unfulfilled sets the terms –
an inspired neutrality squandered on a renewed
sense of strategy imaginatively misapplied.
A punitive ambiguity. Chalked with the sound off.
In what they perceived as a victory over the landscape
the porters first tortured, then killed and ate their prisoner.
An axiom of distributive accretion states: *Termless indices*
deprived of an order of association lack increase.
Wonderment is undermined by modest assertions
and mortal nonchalance. A rare opportunity forlornly
dispersed is a hazardous preoccupation of prolonged thought
with its suggestion of unobstructed outcomes.
Changing perspectives provides no determined plans or prospects.
Among the lesser lights of the constellation no element
of the visionary is displayed in person. Some scruple, or practical
grace, serves as adjunct to the democratic preventative.
Agrippina has prepared the meal. A *poppysma* would not be ill-advised.

8/5/06

Strange stuff, this apprehension in the drag of the pen
across paper – uncomplicated, complicated.
Constituent order, deep structure. Through the dark up ahead.
The greater number of things has replaced the greatest
number of things. The greater number of things has replaced
the greatest number of other things. The greatest number
of things has replaced the greatest number of things.
The greatest number has been replaced by the greater number
of the greatest number. The storm gathers strength.
Simply the words. And the words that are not there. Put there.
The conversation begins with an expression of surprise
that someone is alive. Consider the situation. Consider
the surmise – codes of discretion, incidental decorum aside.
To propound an explanation would ordain a demand.
Clouds pushed by heavy winds overhead cast giant shadows
that drift from west to east across the valley.
The snake not the dog is man's best friend. No one
knows anything. The vagaries of error infect us all.
The pardon indicates unequal halves, equidistant.
What if, above all, what if – what else?
The line projects the base of the angle as far as its vertical side.
But there is no resolve in the angle's assertion because
the base and side ache for further extension. Consider the 4 –
constantly in motion within the confines of infinite vanishing points.
Step forward, move, fall down, move, fall down, move, crawl away.
The snake, not the dog – not simultaneously but intimately.
The plagues are well structured – they begin with trifles.
Camera flashes and yellow leaves. An inward turn,
brief enough for interplay, concocts an alibi.
The poor light confuses the ratio of oil to pigment.
Circumstantial evidence is based on depradations.
In this case a lack of shadows, a gate that was never built.
An ingenious depletion readjusts the subtle effects of the superstition.
What was there? What had been expected? And now with
its presence lost, or deferred, or eclipsed what can be expected?
Tacit accusations swept through the streets of the capital.
Straightening the tower is an ongoing incremental activity.
A span to a cubit, a cubit to a fathom, a fathom to a league.
How many steps to the top depends entirely on the light.
Here the page of the letter turned and the remainder is lost.

8/5 – 6/06

Reserve and suspicion soon gave way to trust and affection.
But the strega, making her telepathic calculations,
had made it clear as she anointed his head with oil –
give your friend an apple, give your enemy a peach.
There was nothing to be gained in rejecting this option
It was to be understood that expediency best serves
the lowest common denominator of motivation and moral choice.
The heaviest burden to be imagined is in the chain of causality
It left him with a renewed sense of the elegiac and querulous
together – both, he believed, in need of further cultivation.
A door hidden in the paneling behind the tapestry slowly opened.
The stone corridors of the chateau were empty,
but he could hear voices coming from the banquet hall.
The strega had spoken of the passage from the Milky Way
ever downward through the seven planets. Now his
concerns were with the accretive nature of the descent
and determining the scope of the *kleroi* – as though he
were making preliminary facets in a roughcut stone
or precisely dated entries in a logbook. Given their moments
of discovery the resulting pages took on a talismanic quality. Emblems
with naked trees, feral dogs, and gutted buildings were predominant.
The ZILZAL, he thought, halted in mid motion.
Or just the rhythm of disclosure?

8/7/06

Before proceeding further, it should be noted, in this case at least,
a noir influence could be plausibly argued. The greatest expert in
these matters spent the last seventeen years of his life in a Calabrian
monastery assembling a compendium of apocalyptic commonplaces.
It was said that a large bird once seized his hair in its beak and
raised him above the earth in order to show him the torments
to follow. He saw a collapsing bridge as it fell in flames into
the rushing waters below. It became a standard symbol in all he wrote.
Obsession, cognition, perception, and expertise, in no particular
order of maintenance – ever more to reveal, ever more to conceal,
weaving a wider net partook of the prospect. Limitations
and losses absolved shaped the liminal peripheries of the vortex.
Calculated options, small risks, self-scrutiny, inward interrogation
repeatedly led not so much to dismay as to further suspicions.
The fabulist opportuned by candor and appeasement –
as well as personal idiosyncrasy. Wound in and out of the light
and unwinding in the strobe – self-rendered as invention.

8/8/06

The sun coasts past the sky. A pair of hands emerge
from the clouds and tear the pages in half.
Divagations – phrases, allusions, attitudes, and gestures –
an amalgam of motives, a name for all, oscillating
along a central axis, arranged as though the fingers and pen
refused to reach the edges of the page.
To begin and end at the source, with an ever more formal
embodiment of independent life summoned at will
and with the unmistaken clarity of grief –
Then I am nothing and only what is infinite.
The starborn distant air suffused with stealth defines
the imponderable, a fatigued desirability confounds the grasp –
all the more reluctant in its anticipation.
With no evidence to the contrary, he found a place
to sit down and allowed his thoughts to take shape.
Nerves of the logos joined as ghosts rounded on the minimal,
intuituiting partition as rudimentary as a vowel, as brief as a syllable –
bleeding away in search of another fastidious success, one
still immured in the whims of burgeoning obscurity.
The coincident dilemmas of gravitas. *What doesn't belong and why*, he wondered?

8/9/06

Hesitant voice and uncertain morale – *acidia* by any other name –
to be put to use. The means from what to what, from where to where,
from when to whereupon? Up to now spatial levels had always determined
distance – and hesitation further confirmed by the proprietary.
But at the moment malevolent events on the frontier, threats and adjustments
mitigated by rivalry, envy, and lack of comprehension plowed the sand.
He stood up, and for a moment extended his arms over his head.
From every angle he looked like someone trying to surrender.
His fingers opened and closed around the heat
of the sun as though it were as palpable as the torn pages.
Behind him in a stepped and pillared building surmounted
by statues of men and animals he could hear the sounds of laughter
and slamming doors. He lowered his arms and sat down again,
listening to the red wind of the *phantastikon pneuma.*
Contemplative aptitude has its perversities –
the yields of the emdash – his self-portrait in paradox:
discreet in confession, not so in action –
a legacy of abandoned voices improved by forgery,
the parts of the equation never alluded to before –
some invoked through invention and others

meant to create bonds and attachments received and
put to use through conscious organization.
Obscurely systematic methods betrayed no sign
of the strangeness of his condition.
Perceived as eager to avenge a fallen leader or loot a caravan
the nomadic carries with it an element of threat.
Inheritors determine the precepts of sect.
The primary directive comes as an instruction to give warning.
How far will the sounds carry? The answer is determined
not by projection but by momentum come to an unexpected stop.
The pieces are moved about on the board with two small
pieces of willow meant to represent the bones of ancestors.

8/10/06

Temples, colonnades, and monuments of such presence
it seemed their ruins exhausted the logic of desire and
had always been thus and had never stood intact.
A habitation without limits or merely a compass point?
He regretted saying what he regretted *not* saying –
not what he regretted *saying*. He was told that the first martyr
had been thrown from the roof of the temple or had leapt
of his own accord. Not many followed despite the passage of years.
A predatory conviction can be read in the whore's smile
as well as the grimace of torture – the resolve
of a simple faith to which little thought was given.
Clouds swallow the moon. The tides still run.
The scythe catches on a stake, pulled away it hits a stone
on the backswing. Birds and murmurs, only midday.
A thick, pugnacious vertical stroke determined a margin –
pressed gently and feathered outward first with the thumb
then carefully finessed and smoothed with the forefinger –
casually contoured so as to suggest motion that had
just ceased or was about to begin again –
trusting the eye to balance a lack of concern for
perfect proportion with the effects of light and shadow.
Out of concern for its natural appearnce did he mean
to say 'undisturbed' or 'unfinished'? Neither a question
nor a solution, but one answer too many.
Paper, pencils, brushes, razor blades, tin cans, charcoal,a reservoir
of turpentine, palette knife, pack of Camels, and a half-smoked cigar
upright in a china cup – little apart from words from which to construct
a fable, precisely lettered in bright yellow and red.

8/11 – 12/06

'O scolglio o altro che nel mare chiuso'.
Part of the letter's missing page was found among
a basketful of embroidered linen on the verandah:
For one more partisan than loyal – and often opportunistic –
the cardinal sign anticipates various crises in the efforts
to establish an equivalence in everyday affairs.
Any appreciable emphasis on the autumn equinox affects
the attempts to reconcile what only paradox validates.
There is a melancholy which accompanies all enthusiasm.
Who's that out the window walking towards the lake?
Along the bottom edge – right or left? Which corner?
Across the back? From bottom to top? – the signature added
as though a spontaneous afterthought – but now considered
necessary to complete the image of the renewed urgency of
the climb – a careful assessment of autumn light, sea, and foliage.
Hieroglyphics, calligraphy, scribes, and pickpockets.
Even a liar prefers those around him to tell the truth.
The only other window in the room faced the street.
Cenno, cenni. 'E di ciò fanno bene'. Mais, tortura, QUID TUM?

8/13/06

Nothing more than objects with names opposing the functions
they serve – surrendered to the gods of the street:
today the earth is flat and the room is round,
tomorrow the earth is less flat and the room is still round,
the next day the earth is round and the room is empty.
"It was only yesterday – have you forgotten already?"
"Yes, but have you forgotten yesterday was Sunday?"
Pushed by a gentle breeze, how does one establish
the exact moment when everything that has already
happened was, though meticulously managed, merely
prologue – since *how* unavoidably nuances *where* and *when?*
And the habit of nuance is complicit with *why* – as well as *why not.*
He wanted to answer but he was dressed in rags and could
no longer determine even the day of the week, knowing
only that it had once been Sunday – its incongruity
lured into disintegration. Tuning Belacqua's lute, sound
echoes in sound mimicking the pause to look, turn,
and look again. He returns a jar filled with pieces of
broken glass, old coins, and bird bones to a niche in the cave wall.
Elementary diversions, intrinsic offenses, compulsory suspicions
coaxed from invented names – real pleasures. Snow in August.

8/14 – 15/06

The tips of the index finger and thumb are joined together
and then separated by the index finger of the other hand.
From Job to the Evangelists, *uno pernacchio sconfinato,*
darkness, weeping, hunger, stench, fire, the worm, ruins, scatter,
and despair, *l'abbraccio smagrito di disprezzo – ora, domani, passato,*
and beyond the measure of time – points of reference,
points of departure, made entirely of ghosts, apocrypha, and
false attributions – interrupted again and again. *Curved like a scythe*
the index finger is dragged across the forehead from left to right.
Or so *tutti gli scribacchiatori* will think who retell these things.

8/16/06

salt in the rock

NOTEBOOKS
NOVEMBER–DECEMBER, 2008

A PATTERN OF DAYS

By writing he escaped from the world into the natural world of the mind.

The word must be put down for itself, not as a symbol of nature but a part, cognizant of the whole – aware – civilized.
                                                    —William Carlos Williams

Only a small part of what is said can be verified.
                                                    —Beckett

11/1/08

Subtract a few
to add a few elsewhere
Add a few
and add a few elsewhere
[No refrain]

Un Aller En Avant
Icones Symbolica
In the security of
A conjectured labyrinth

Names, attributes, dignities

Ars Combinandi
Points of contact:
Work out of work into
work out of work

The Treatise
the confiscation
the reply – perfecting
the proportions by the assurances of number

The measure measured

Absent exegetical methods [vanity]
Grammar, Poetry, Memory,
Mathematics, ethics
Containment, shifts of light and shadow

Diapase

Thought is perpetual misgiving
Hence the persistence of thought

Experimental content
mounting to disclosure
The telling of the telling
within the disclosure

Syntactic scaffolding
Apart from memory's intent
Not an imagined
but an availed image *opportuning*
What news from the palimpsest?

Language in profile
Language simultaneously
In relief

Sound's geometry
Speech shaped
by occasions of language
– not the reverse

11/11/08

Memory preserves what desire cannot sustain.

The accomplishment
of the amalgam
is found in the marginal

Pages steadied by the layers
of contrast measuring the allusions
turned within and against
the more shadowy margins

Mistaking the dissolving clouds
for the shifting light

The inconsequence of detail without nuance
An exhausted stoicism and weary irony

Alchemizing appraisals
into something immediate

Insistence and deferral
repeated endlessly
within and beyond crisis

Because of its expression
or because of its *claims*?

Stripping the illusory of its devices:
the unremarkable and the avid

Taken from the declining peripheries –

Nothing left to be given away

11/20/08

Fate provides what Providence only discloses.

The elimination of historical presumptions

Transparencies: Rites of Pallor

Take the first street on *the* right
and then the last on *your* left.

The blind, the hallucinated, the idiosyncratic
rising with the stars

Blotting-paper testimony:
Habit is discussed by Hegel.
Habit may relieve some of the weight
of everyday life, but it holds the mind
back from the threshold of freedom.

Millions of answers blown hard on the coals –

Phantom statutes and the addition
of endangered material implying speed

The unnatural calm of an empty cage

Now all that remain are the valorized
longer passages – inescapable weavings,
false eruptions, furtive manufactories,
subsidiary posts, pointless attractions,
breakdown composites of conventional
exchanges . . . never ending curves

Insignificant spaces lined with cork –
dry as the moon
and as happy to oblige

Rock-crystal, papyrus, black sand, and sawdust
– against the recoverable

Jeux-de-mots: skin

[Head lowered] [Contextual italic]
Talks aloud to himself as accurately and distinctly as possible

11/24/08

TRANSCENDENTAL ANECDOTES

Death of a Man Killed by a Snake

He dies of grief and his soul haunts the city.
[Art and Love in Renaissance Italy]

No conventional values – NO values –
along the dreamroad
– only curvature and Euclidian shadows

What the vigilant have placed there

A given circumstance: the inheritance
of disobedience and misdemeanor

Only a few people would follow his coffin
to the cemetery – none of them had he numbered
among his friends – they were the tail of the lizard

Resignation / No doubt
Mild submission / Special appeal

A logic that transcends any system
A biological pastime

No recognizable traits
invented creatures improved by peculiar flourishes –
gestures made by swinging the left arm over the head
once or twice and then bringing it stiffly
to the side of the body – like a salute

Standing in the middle of a circle

Diminutives: impersonating the dead

To understand but never comprehend

33 Diameters –
No circumference
Rapid motions, frosty vapors
Mirth in the cruel rebuke

The music stops, the smile burns, a turn to the left

11/27/08

Politics: The pursuit of the partially informed with the ill-conceived

Speechless: Similarly vented
Subsequent: Aimlessly subsequent
Position: whether
Wether: Its position
Reasoning: That notion
Another thought: This other thought on its own

Raining the last time
Always winter
The last time
[The turning point]

Words are many
The first fiasco
Words are few
The next fiasco
Words are many
The last fiasco

Back and forth like a grin

No such thing as one
No such one

Backing away – holding aloft

You have nothing
You have to say yes to everything

The poem and its registers
The painting and its registers
The registers and their registers

Metaphor's memory
Metaphor remembering
Memory's metaphor

11/30/08

Saying not what is
But what becomes

Banged up
Face down
Turns out
[Leaving an impression]

Conspiracy
Burglary
Aggravated assault
Kidnapping
Unlawful restraint
[How it turned out]

Conspiracy, aggravated assault, unlawful restraint, text

The birds quit
The birds quit the moon
The birds quit
The birds quit
The birds quit the moon
The birds quit
The birds squat
Quitters
The birds squat
The birds squat on the moon
                    —Birdsong

You hear
You doubt you heard it
You heard it
You hear it again

Marked with an accent
Meaning changes
An alternative world
Of wind and rain
– The *duello* its code

12/3/08

[Spandrel]

Bermerkungen – this and that obiter
proposing, dissembling, proposing, dissembling . . .

Thinking utterance thinking color of that color
in this aspect or that

Color of this color
color of that
differentiated into obscurity
differentiated into exclusion

One and the other
one *of* the other
Emphasis inclined to circumstance –
a practical reliance on exhausted justifications

Charmed, confused, obedient –
I am inclined to say
In a low voice, without moving
keeping a steady distance

Nothing was lost

I had been invited to stand here to spend the evening
so to speak to stand here and say whatever came to mind –
whatever the hour and the effort allowed – whatever
standing here enabled – it had been an invitation extended
by someone I didn't know but who knew I wouldn't refuse

Screws it open screws it shut and there revealed was his
great awareness giving way to either at any given moment
open or shut sometimes with one hand tucked behind him
sometimes the left sometimes the right he assumed full
responsibility for his choices left hand behind and screws
it shut right hand behind and screws it open and so on
his choice always open or shut left hand or right thus
some or many were amazed

[Bas-de-page]

12/4/08

[Pictogram]

Though always secondary
such excesses make myth relevant
if not central

A bird barks and an eager dog whines
– the subversion of fruitful inquiry

Tempos of uncertainty without ironic purpose

Corrosion and the lived experience informing ideology

As nuanced as any anticipated dialectic –
however fugitive the lexical foundation

Deliberated, calculated, structured, and advanced –
still without any assurance of comprehension or successful conviction
– only the achievement of a decisive polarity

Where we: You or I or you *and* I
can and cannot go

Recusant cohesion for some and an utter confusion of details
prior, during, and after for others

Nothing else to be done
nothing else to say
nothing else (reservedly) to add

Left to some future stiff breeze to connive

12/7/08

INKHARD: A DISCURSIVE CONJECTURE

An isolated system of possibilities
Mythical entities of our own invention
An awareness already possessed but rejected in favor of painful contradictions

No theories are required in pursuit of some form of justification

Nothing is hidden – everything essential is invisible

Utterance as if from a reservoir

Distorted by the illusory no matter how
well aimed or sharing in agreements – morphing
an hermeneutic out of the a priori
– coerced into the order of attentions

Analogous to that which we speak of –
the uses of attention
the uses of concern

In accordance with a finite regression of interpretations
– Bring back to words
words back from –
featured in their circumstance beyond contextual detail

To attribute we invent

We invent to attribute to invention the extent we attribute

Responses intrinsically unpredictable and indeterminate
in their grasp of the hidden

12/10/08

Spawls and vraic

Artisal compensation for the speechless object

To penetrate the exact with the offhand
Forward moving, spatially limited, absorbed into the record

What was and what is
– Kicked into a splash –
The ambiguity of the results does not tolerate any constraint

Impatient imitation of every nuance

The tenacity of designation, the consequent excision
Shrinking sounds
The relevance of ends that are unknown

Those who don't pay hear nothing

A token tenaciously preserved hangs on the wall
waits for someone to approach –
The primordial affect: what is to be heard/seen
and safeguarded as a possession

A sound that *inhabits*
The anonymous truth-content of sound
Mouthpiece then horn

Voice fails to require physical appearance in order to remain its abstraction

When reproduction breaks down objects are transformed

THE ONE ITSELF spinning in its own orbit

Achievements not necessarily humane, achievements nonetheless

Flattering [adj] ideologies

Its height and its abyss [Adorno]

Stasis tied to time and place
Stasis placed in time and recollected
The antithesis of movement composed

Explores and resides
Inseparably committed

Justification submerged in compulsion rescues the justification

A strategic reversal at the price of immediacy

Hesitantly entered by means of a detour

To capture extended durations where they converge

Distanced and often conventionalized at the expense of their substance

Unmediated compositional form
Objectification liked to perception
Blissful moments become fatal

Ritual as a form of sound – the *pause* of expectation already sobered

Extramusical loci whose purposes remain unknown
despite thematic determinations conditioned
and varied by the performative aspect

The improvisational reverses the improvisatory

The essential opportunity [real or imagined] and the articulation of its duration

Private disclosures resisting social rituals redefine boundaries
– The reactionary neutralizes process

Complexity manifesting the wealth within as well as the power to exclude

Between the contorted body and the spectacle/celebration of gesture
– The ludic directed inward

The score: historiated pen-flourishes
Figures assembled for glossing

The minute delineations devoted to the unseen
The inchoate interstices of the unseeable – untamed voussoirs

Set along and against the edges
fleshy and fragmentary

Finding no impetus
apart from the recuperative
in the status quo

The anxiety of enumeration –
silence and excited grunts

The unfinished body

A cacophony enlarging the vernacular

Real referents – a rabble – *protrude*

Conscious, willful usurpations

12/12/08

Stone prong and metal ring – in accordance with –

One set within the other – a beginning, a complexity

A lock of shadows poised to gather and point
– awaiting the slackened obscenity of a heavy body

Attendant with a murderous pull the chain completes

Recreant – the fugue falls in upon its shimmering
coaxed into an interrogatory order

The status of the quo and the status of the qua
among the deepening shades

Words are many
the standard wicking
– the squeeze of the mud

North shadow east shadow south shadow
no shadow unaccountable darkness

The glare of the sun in a shadowless desert valley

THE CONVERSATION: *Saying nothing is a characteristic expression
of life, a life many might even prefer depending on their disposition
and the assessment made of any obstacles that might prevent the accurate
determinations of distances or whatever else might appear threatened –*

The forms selected and the shapes
into which they are altered –
neither meta nor physical but circumstantial

Triste redux: Incubus with a flute, succubus with a drum

Subsequent interests included spontaneous action and etymology

No new way out only another way around

Meridians of the Long March

Derived and soon populated

Derelict, diegetic or non diegetic [Formal ploys]

Not Progress
Not Presence
But Present Progressive

EUPHORIC GLOAMING
Grey skies
grey sea
black line
lacking the span of the horizon

MUMOUR
Names
The place
Place
The names

WITHON
Out within the without
In without the within
In within the without
Out within the within

Masque, masqua, masqualm

Brewing climate, schematized vistas, lurching
foliage, recursive arcs, abandoned interiors

Lowered ceiling / Opposite pages

Stubborn pigment suggesting the failed gravitas of uncertain provenance

Peach hues and muffled sounds
– every brushstroke proposes parallels
Process complicated by equivalence

Insistence and duration
Insistence and duration
Insistence and duration

Duration and insistence
Duration and insistence
Duration and insistence

Insistence and insistence
Duration and duration
And insistence and duration

Duration and duration
Insistence and insistence
And duration and duration

Insistence and duration
Insistence and duration
Insistence and duration
Insistence and duration
Insistence and duration
Insistence and duration
Insistence and duration
Insistence and duration

12/15/08

Formula and Meaning / Figures and Associations

What leads forth – read as derivation

Panoramic SEMA TAWY

Visual inquiry, deployed motifs

Billows above flagstone patterns

Sinking into the distance
filling the distance
creating the distance

Instead of proximity – *definition*

Landscape refined to epigram

A complicated dexterity – in front of a dead animal –
Encounter scenes, panels, and graphic clues
Formulaic textures and unmediated formats
Designations not merely illustrative

Extraction lacking autonomy given the placement
and careful arrangement of persistent detail

THEODOLITHIC WALL RELIEF
Idioms of chiasmus
Oppositional Emblems
Longitudinal axes
Subsidiary representations
Reluctant immanence

PRECEDENCE [Empire]
Against an expanding panorama

12/17/08

What are you doing? What are you becoming? -Sonia Delaunay

A thought, comment, or musical phrase
– signed and then fastened with a large paper and wax seal.

Stability and cohesion–the attraction
of any allusion, an occasion in which
to offer proof in a secretarial hand . . .

Gilded Rigors – time consuming and often hazardous –
A material witness 18 inches high

Andante – intended to mark and end

Moon – Weariness
Water – Fleetingness
Rose – Beauty

Halfway around the hoop: what started what else?

A blast of yellow lights
Ice-bound at the margins of the page

YOUR LETTER OF 15TH ULTIMO
There were
these words
left here

And there were
these words
left here

Other's opinions had not been unexpected
even when what was involved was compiling
a list determined by certain arbitrary limitations
numbers, words, or numbers of words, the ordering
a factor of small enterprise and self-betraying incentive
when sleep failed to come or offer some resolution
to what had been too difficult to consider head on –

A sensual temperament betrayed by a hypersensitive conscience

Described and transformed thereby
– but without leaving any trace behind

Unpredictable basic elements now beyond emphasis or explanation

A fountain, a glass ball, three wicker chairs
There had been a garden
—there will be a garden

The exact number of pages—
the limit beyond which no one can go until
the pattern loses focus and begins to blur

THE MESSENGER IN THE MEZZANINE
Resentment: Condoned
Tribal animosity: condoned
Execration: condoned
Demoralization: condoned
Torture: condoned
Massacre: condoned
Anarchy: condoned

Almost nothing
—something falling—
a claustrophobic blankness
—remaining, scrutinized

Torpor's various heralds
staring out into the darkness
waiting for purpose—

The watchman is ringing his bell, I therefore must conclude . . .

Mark this—
plug the gaps with seamless gestures

Mark this
if you think its fate
is to tell you
something you don't
already know

The aesthetic:
a shared confidence

12/20/08

THE UNSILVERED GLASS

A perished indignation has given
way to a mistaken sense of the virtuous

High and low numbers added together
and divided by a reluctant quantity

We see so little—
allow me to add to that
reaching up out of the smoking ruins

Disinclination extends from door to door

Indisposition, secret anger, indiscretion,
discontent, scrupulously cultivated

Punctuality, accuracy, and precision

Composure and the conciliatory
to the point of martyrdom

Subtly circular
—wafted by a slight breeze

Inwardly accessible
only on foot

12/21/08

Fragments on all sides –
a sensible loss

A form of commonwealth
from without as well as from within

A mechanical readjustment
– back the way they had come

Every deafmute a foreigner
clapping and humming
humming an clapping
shakes hands arguing the point
– consuming most of what he'd rather share

In my time the ashes were *this* high
and covered the statues up to their eyes

Historia Calamitatum
More by example than by words

Distraction – no more than distressed concentration

Fascination turning into legibility
Whence the awkward pleasure

The paradox in the short term –
its perfected closure spoiled by an ill-considered apology

Risen from a lower world
Hence no longer astonished

12/22/08

SPHINXKNOT

The last word
The game stops –
The next word

Frozen in smoke
– backlit

The avowal endlessly glossed –
The demand does not *align*

Something intimate desired of its employment

Broken apart [controlled]
Remains standing [unspoken]

Expenditures
that leave a mark
Expenditures that don't
Both dilemmas situate
within the formula

The voice when it
reaches me is not
the voice you hear
but the voice you
would apprehend

Done in the dark
with no expectation
of light or any other
expenditure of awareness
within the frailty of form

All written form
is resolved in comedic
evanescence blunted
by terror and pity

12/23/08

Every striving for meaning begins in remorse
isolated from what its durance would determine and sustain
in an intractable affirmation of its recourse to solitude

Simulation restored to the psychological
– a connivance with every rhetorical strategy
plotting against the speaker

The quest for sense assumes an acceptation
of a failed instrument of distancing
– a reservoir of injunctions within the uses of the anxiety of argument

– mimicry and legend, labor and tribal displeasure –
suggesting posture or p.o.v.?

What one says of
in abandoning a need to know

Indifference aids and unmasks

Subject and object embrace their discovery within the prerogative
Intervals – as motionless and extended as music –
metonymic in their absence

Form become fetish

One abandons what to return to what

An expenditure – a transformative concession
separating the alternative from the discrete agreement
sealing the initiative

Interpretive impulses
shaping/anticipating
a remainder, an identity
[held close, taken up]

Successful modes of affect sustain demand
and provide further illusory notions of opportunity

Asks the same question – offers the same answer
Asks of the answer a different question – attaches a different answer to it

WITNESS TO THE DRY SPELL
Rain –
but only as described

Only inadvertence
– not conceptual
merely literal

Absence: inhabited, uninhabited

Inscribed within every speculative assertion
Is a melancholy disequilibrium in which
Anxious complicity stakes its violence

What I hide with my body my language utters

Reassured by the illusion of control
And the coercive nature of form
The checked impulse survives as perpetual mutability

Doubts and refinements beyond these terms

12/27/08

The House of Blue Lights – and these its 18 rooms

The flux of schema
the acquisitive calculus

– This is all hypothetical, he said, for our unanticipated purposes.

Relevance – if not consistency

Something odd in counting beyond application:
red, blue, green, yellow, black, white divided by
what is tensed in the future probable

Shaded along a straight line
a combining that devalorizes the function of memory
– or the elegiac

What has been lifted from an angle

Expectation establishes a willed occurrence corresponding
to one or more irreducible/nonspecific assertions whose
position and scope have been fixed by their moment
to reach in various directions – an amorphous series of
finite aggregates in infinite combinations implying
the heterological shaded along a curved line

Other Titles from Otis Books / Seismicity Editions

J. Reuben Appelman, *Make Loneliness*
    Published 2008 | 84 pages | $12.95
    ISBN-10: 0-9796177-0-7
    ISBN-13: 978-0-9796177-0-6

Guy Bennett and Béatrice Mousli, Editors, *Seeing Los Angeles:*
    A Different Look at a Different City
    Published 2007 | 202 pages | $12.95
    ISBN-10: 0-9755924-9-1
    ISBN-13: 978-0-9755924-9-6

Jean-Michel Espitallier, *Espitallier's Theorem*
    Translated from the French by Guy Bennett
    Published 2003 | 137 pages | $12.95
    ISBN: 0-9755924-2-4

Norman M. Klein, *Freud in Coney Island and Other Tales*
    Published 2006 | 104 pages | $12.95
    ISBN: 0-9755924-6-7

Ken McCullough, *Left Hand*
    Published 2004 | 191 pages | $12.95
    ISBN: 0-9755924-1-6

Béatrice Mousli, Editor, *Review of Two Worlds: French and American*
    Poetry in Translation
    Published 2005 | 148 pages | $12.95
    ISBN: 0-9755924-3-2

Ryan Murphy, *Down with the Ship*
    Published 2006 | 66 pages | $12.95
    ISBN: 0-9755924-5-9

Eric Priestley, *For Keeps*
    Published 2009 | 264 pages | $12.95
    ISBN-13: 978-0-979-6177-4-4
    ISBN-10: 0-9796177-4-X

Hélène Sanguinetti, *Hence This Cradle*
    Translated from the French by Ann Cefola
    Published 2007 | 160 pages | $12.95
    ISBN: 970-0-9755924-7-2

Janet Sarbanes, *Army of One*
  Published 2008 | 173 pages | $12.95
  ISBN-10: 0-9796177-1-5
  ISBN-13: 978-0-9796177-1-3

Severo Sarduy, *Beach Birds*
  Translated from the Spanish by Suzanne Jill Levine
      and Carol Maier
  Published 2007 | 182 pages | $12.95
  ISBN: 978-9755924-8-9

Adriano Spatola, *Toward Total Poetry*
  Translated from the Italian by Brendan W. Hennessey
      and Guy Bennett
  with an Introduction by Guy Bennett
  Published 2008 | 176 pages | $12.95
  ISBN: 978-0-9796177-2-0, 0-9796177-3-1

Carol Treadwell, *Spots and Trouble Spots*
  Published 2004 | 176 pages | $12.95
  ISBN: 0-9755924-0-8

Allyssa Wolf, *Vaudeville*
  Published 2006 | 82 pages | $12.95
  ISBN: 0-9755924-4-0

Forthcoming in 2009–2010

Bruce Bégout, *Common Place. The American Motel.*

Sophie Rachmul, *Los Angeles 1950–1990 – The Emergence of an Artistic Scene and of a Poetic Discourse on the City.*